An Early Start to Science

Roy Richards
Margaret Collis
Doug Kincaid

And these coffee stains are here to "break-in" the book for you - as I unconsciously drenched it while reading.

Macdonald Educational

First published in Great Britain in 1987 by
Macdonald & Co (Publishers) Ltd
Reprinted 1987 (with amendment), 1988, 1989

This impression published by
Macdonald Educational
Simon & Schuster International Group
Wolsey House, Wolsey Road
Hemel Hempstead HP2 4SS

Printed and bound in Great Britain by
Purnell Book Production Ltd

British Library Cataloguing in Publication Data

Richards, Roy
    An early start to science
    1. Science—Study and teaching (Elementary)
    I. Title II. Collis, Margaret III. Kincaid, Doug
    372.3'5 LB1585
    ISBN 0-356-11555-0

Edited by John Day
Designed by Jerry Watkiss and David Bryant/Joan Farmer Artists
Artwork by David Bryant/Joan Farmer Artists
Production by Ken Holt

ACKNOWLEDGEMENTS
The authors and publishers warmly thank the staff and
children of The Rachel McMillan Nursery School for their
generous help in producing the photographs on pages 26–28.

They also thank SCDC Publications for its kind permission to
reproduce on page 4 the Basic Ideas in Science list, first
published in *Learning Through Science: Guide and Index.*

This book provides a wealth of experiences of a scientific nature for young children. These make it clear that science for young children should not consist of an easier version of secondary school practice but rather be an extension of the primary drives present in active five-year-olds. That is to say:

☐ *exploration of their immediate environment in order to gather experiences at first hand*

☐ *manipulation of objects and materials*

☐ *observation of the things around them*

☐ *comparison of things, one with another*

☐ *questioning and arguing about things*

☐ *testing things out, indulging in simple problem solving activities*

Developing these skills should help the children in their acquisition of knowledge, increase their vocabulary and communication skills, and help them to develop an awareness, interest and concern for the animate and inanimate things of their world.

The illustrations in the text show the objects that need to be collected, the vast majority of which are the ordinary, everyday bits and pieces that lie around the children. This is not only because they are cheap but also because they are the things that are meaningful to children and most easily help in the task of bringing about understanding. The experiences suggested should fit easily into the context of first-school practice and a glance through the book will show that we very much intend a strong dialogue between teacher and children. It is a voyage of discovery by the children where the teacher's role is crucial, and all will come to nought unless that discovery is guided. We have tried hard to show the nature of that guidance, to remain within the world of young children and the wonders and enjoyment of that world. Bon voyage.

Basic ideas in science

Concept development comes slowly, some concepts being more difficult to understand than others. The basis for understanding scientific concepts is found in the wealth of experience set out in this book. Using the book and its forthcoming companion volume *An Early Start to Nature*, we would say that children should gain experience of most of the basic ideas set out in the list below. It comes from the *Guide and Index* to Learning Through Science.

Interdependence   Living things depend on each other in various ways.

Food chains   Some animals eat plants and some eat other animals but all animals ultimately depend on green plants.

Adaptation   Living things are usually well suited in form and function to their natural environment.

Variation   No two living things are identical in all respects. Even within one species there are differences.

Life needs   Most living things need water, air and nourishment for life processes.

Growth and development   Living things grow and develop and these require food.

Reproduction   Living things produce offspring of the same kind.

Life cycle   Living things of the same kind go through the same life cycle.

Sensitivity   Living things are sensitive to their environment. They respond to stimuli. They move in various ways.

Senses   In humans the senses are sight, touch, hearing, taste and smell which each provide different information about the environment.

Classification   Animals, plants and materials can be sorted on the basis of different criteria into groups, sets or collections.

Environment   In any situation there are many variable conditions all in operation at the same time. These can affect and modify places and their inhabitants.

Weather   This is the atmospheric conditions prevailing in a place at a given time.

Atmosphere   There is air around the earth which contains the oxygen that living things need. It also contains water vapour, some of which condenses out in various conditions to give rain, dew, mist, snow, ice or water. It has mass.

Seasons   Changes in the physical environment due to seasonal cycles are often matched by changes or events in the living world.

Soil   Soil is a mixture of things coming from rocks and living things. Substances taken from the soil by plants during growth must be replaced to maintain fertility.

Solar system   The apparent movements of the sun, moon and stars follow a regular pattern.

Forces   To make anything move (or change the way it moves) there has to be a force (push, pull or twist) acting on it.

Friction   This is the resistance which a body meets when moving over a surface or through a gas or liquid.

Strength of things   The strength of an object or structure depends on its shape and on the material of which it is made.

Pressure   This is the force exerted over unit area. The larger the area over which a force is spread, the smaller the force on each unit part.

Water   Water varies in hardness and acidity and can be affected by various agents. It can be absorbed by some materials. It tends to flow until its surface reaches a common level.

Floating and sinking   Whether an object floats or sinks depends on the substance of which it is made and on its shape and on the properties of the liquid. Objects completely immersed in a liquid displace a volume of liquid equal to their own volume.

Energy sources   There is a variety of sources of energy such as food, fuel, moving air, moving water, stretched springs and chemicals.

The 'go' of things   Energy is required for things to move. The faster an object is moving, the more energy it has.

Energy required for change   Energy (often in the form of heat) is required for such changes as melting and evaporation to take place.

States of matter   In general, a substance can be classified either as a solid or a liquid or a gas.

Changes of state   The processes of melting, freezing, evaporating and condensing do not change what a substance is made of.

Change   Change does not 'just happen' but always results from some interaction.

Conservation   This is the idea that the total quantity of a thing is invariable.

Magnetism   Magnets attract and repel other magnets and attract magnetic substances. This power is called magnetism.

Electric circuit   A complete circuit of conducting material is needed for a steady current to flow between the terminals of a battery.

Gravity   All things are pulled towards the earth. Gravity is the force which makes them feel heavy. The balance and stability of things are affected by this force.

Light   Objects can be seen because of the light which they give out or reflect. Light travels (in a uniform medium) in straight paths or rays.

Sound   Sound comes from vibrating objects. Variations in properties such as the length, thickness, tautness and material of the object can change the sound.

Solubility   Some substances dissolve in water. Others do not, but may dissolve in other liquids.

Time, distance, speed   Time is the duration of an event. Distance is the measure of the interval between two points. The speed of an object depends on the distance it travels in a certain time.

Area   Area is the amount of surface covered.

Volume   This is the measure of space occupied by a three-dimensional object.

Space and shape   There are horizontal, vertical and other directional ways of exploring space and shapes.

Mass   A measure of the amount of 'stuff' in an object.

Weight   Weight is a measure of the amount of pull by the earth on an object.

Density   The mass of unit volume of a substance.

Temperature   Temperature is a measure of hotness.

Machine   A device that enables work to be done more quickly or more easily.

Materials   The properties of different materials fit them for different functions.

Children are fascinated by things about themselves and their friends. A good start to work on this topic can be made by looking at the whole body.

One child draws around another

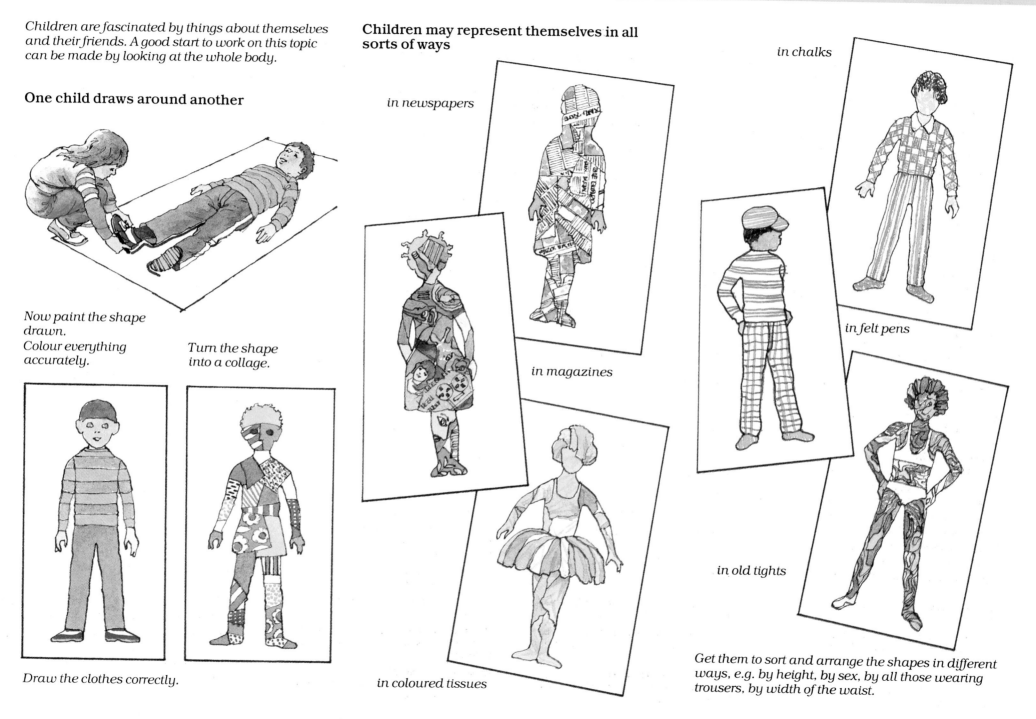

Now paint the shape drawn.
Colour everything accurately.

Turn the shape into a collage.

Draw the clothes correctly.

Children may represent themselves in all sorts of ways

in newspapers

in magazines

in coloured tissues

in chalks

in felt pens

in old tights

Get them to sort and arrange the shapes in different ways, e.g. by height, by sex, by all those wearing trousers, by width of the waist.

Make some handprints

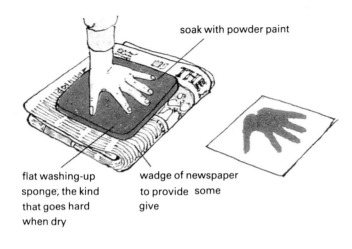

soak with powder paint

flat washing-up sponge; the kind that goes hard when dry

wadge of newspaper to provide some give

Keep experimenting until you get a good print.

Cut out and colour a hand shape

black and white

multi-coloured

tones of one colour

Hang them up in order of size.

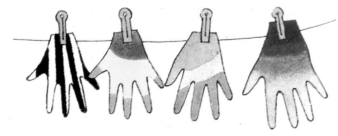

Is this order the same as the order of heights?

Make some hand drawings

Ask children to draw around a friend's hand.

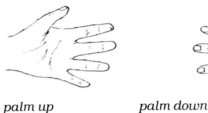

palm up   *palm down*

Get them to draw what they see on their hands. Compare these with the printed examples.

Measure the area of your hand

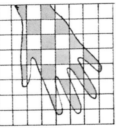

Display the results in a way that draws attention. Does the hand with the widest span cover the most area?

Make some long finger puppets

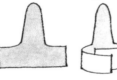

Cut shapes to fit the longest finger. Leave flaps at the side for fixing at the back.

Decorate.

Display the finished puppets.

Is the child with the longest finger puppet, the tallest?

Make some fingerprints

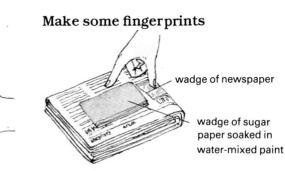

wadge of newspaper

wadge of sugar paper soaked in water-mixed paint

There are four kinds:

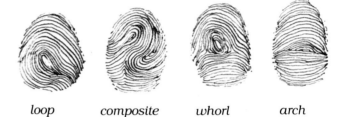

loop   *composite*   *whorl*   *arch*

Print on other materials, such as thin cotton. Here are some design ideas.

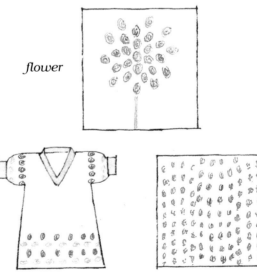

flower

pattern for a printed dress

pattern for a wallpaper

Make some footprints

Do this in the same way as for hand prints.

Don't forget the bowl for washing.

Look at the shapes you get.

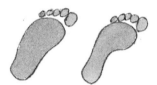

How many are like each of these?

Walk along a strip of kitchen paper.

Run along a strip of kitchen paper.

Which part of the foot touches the ground when you walk?
Which part of the foot touches the ground when you run?

Make up a movement sequence

What do you think this one shows?

Make up other sequences.

Feet and shoes

Make more footprints (left and right). Cut them out.
Draw around your shoes (left and right).
Cut out the shoe shapes.
Put the footprints on the shoe shapes.

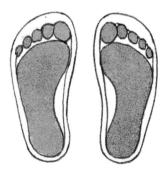

How well do they fit?
Do the footprints overlap the shoes?
Do the shoes seem big enough?

Draw around some feet

Make some measurements. Keep a careful record

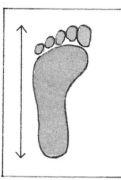 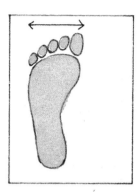

length   *width*

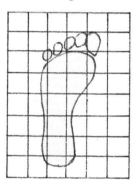 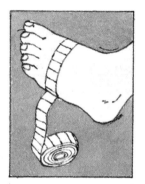

area   *girth*

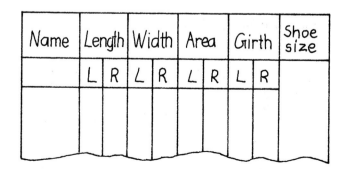

Name	Length		Width		Area		Girth		Shoe size
	L	R	L	R	L	R	L	R	

Do taller children have larger, wider feet?

Look carefully at eyes

Draw, colour and cut out pairs of eyes. Sort them and then mount them as a chart.

blue grey brown hazel

Feeling and listening

Guess what objects are when they are placed in the hand. Use touch alone.

Hide all sorts of objects in tins. Can children guess what is in the tins by tumbling and shaking them in the hand?

Put in
a coin
a pin
a pencil
a rubber
a feather
a sweet
sand.

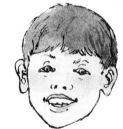

Look at ears

Some have prominent ear lobes.

Some have fixed ear lobes.

How many of each are there in the class?

Talk about noses

Some are prominent.
Some are pointed.
Some are broad.
Some are snubbed.
Guess what types of nose these are.

Smelling

Select four things to guess by smell alone. Now try a different four. Are the things we are most familiar with, the easiest to guess?
Pick a distinctive range, e.g. tea, chocolate, perfume, banana, coffee, apple, cheese, vinegar, spices.

Is it easier to guess if the things are wet?

Talk about tongues

Who has the largest tongue?

How many children can fold their tongues this way?

Tasting

Crunchy things such as carrot, swede, turnip and raw potato are good for taste tests. Try pears, apples, bananas and other fruit, too. Crisps come in lots of flavours.
Texture often gives too strong a clue; it makes for a fairer test if all food is finely chopped.
Try tomato sauce, salt, lemon, tea, coffee and onions, too.
Try holding your nose and tasting things.

Blindfold a child

Remove his or her jacket.
Now test the child.

What colour is the jacket?
How many buttons has it got?
Has it got a top pocket?
Are there any buttons on the sleeves?
How many pockets has it got?
What is in the right pocket?
What is in the left pocket?
Are there any badges pinned on?

Can a blindfolded child find his or her way to the teacher's desk?
Start from the back of the room.
Take care!

Draw or write with eyes covered.

Get the children to stand in a circle.
Choose a child to stand at the centre.
Blindfold the child. Can she or he touch Jim? Joan? Leroy?

Can you walk straight when you can't see?

Draw a straight line across the playground.
Let each child have three goes.
Plot the path with chalk.

first try

second try

third try

Do people tend to move to the right or to the left or do they walk straight?

Who can see furthest?

Arrange a row of pictures at one end of the school hall. Test the children in turn. Let each advance until he or she can name all the pictures correctly.
Measure the distance of each child from the pictures. The greater the distance, the better the vision.

Collect things you can see through

Discuss the difference between transparent, translucent and opaque objects.

Which is the most popular colour in the class?

Make surveys and record the results.

How many colours can you see:
in the classroom
in a picture book
being worn
in the garden
on stamps
out in the street?

Persistence of vision

Draw a fish on one side of a piece of card and a bowl on the other. Put it in the split end of a cane. Spin it.

Collect and make things that make sounds

Yoghurt cartons

A noise like horses' hooves.

Use the cartons and some seeds to make a shaker.

bind together with tape

Glass jars and wine glasses

Add water to the containers to change the pitch. Use a variety of containers to get a good range of pitches.

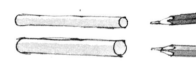

Use pencils and dowel rods as strikers.

Bottles

Blow across the tops.

What gives a high note?
What gives a low note?
What gives a loud sound?
What gives a quiet sound?

Try playing some tunes. Make up some songs.

Shakers

Use peas, beans, rice, sugar, gravel, marbles in the containers.

Pluckers

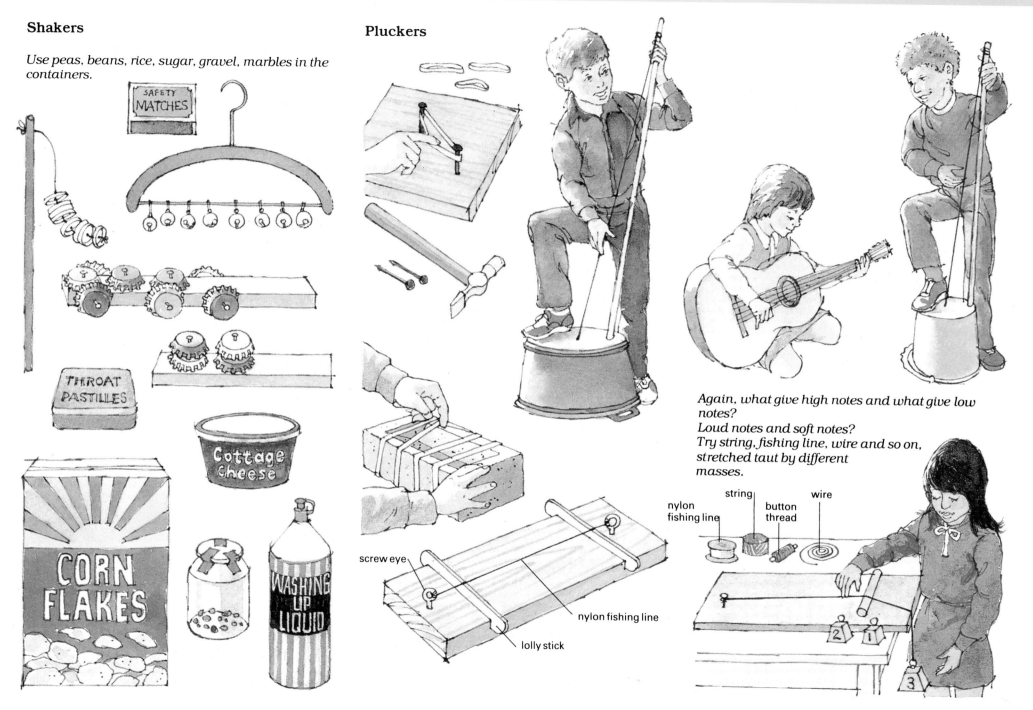

Again, what give high notes and what give low notes?
Loud notes and soft notes?
Try string, fishing line, wire and so on, stretched taut by different masses.

SAFETY MATCHES

THROAT PASTILLES

Cottage Cheese

CORN FLAKES

WASHING UP LIQUID

screw eye

nylon fishing line

lolly stick

nylon fishing line

string

button thread

wire

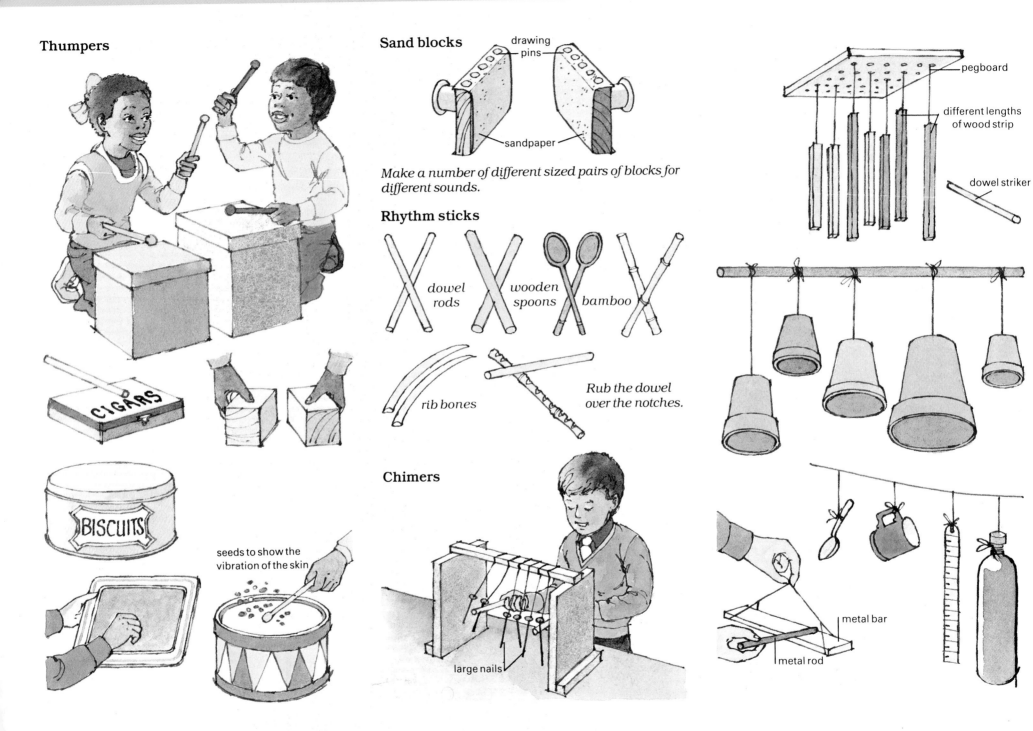

Thumpers

CIGARS

BISCUITS

seeds to show the vibration of the skin

Sand blocks

drawing pins

sandpaper

Make a number of different sized pairs of blocks for different sounds.

Rhythm sticks

dowel rods

wooden spoons

bamboo

rib bones

Rub the dowel over the notches.

Chimers

large nails

pegboard

different lengths of wood strip

dowel striker

metal bar

metal rod

Tin can telephone
Sound travelling through string.

thin tin can

matchstick

Card megaphone
Sound channelled in one direction through air.

Speaking tube
Sound travelling through air.

funnel

garden hose

Jangling spoons
Sound travelling through string.

How far away can you hear the ticking watch?

Balloon full of water
Sound travelling through water.

Dowel rod inserted into a funnel
Sound travelling through wood.

Ticking watch
Sound travelling through wood.

Collect seeds

These seeds are easy to grow.

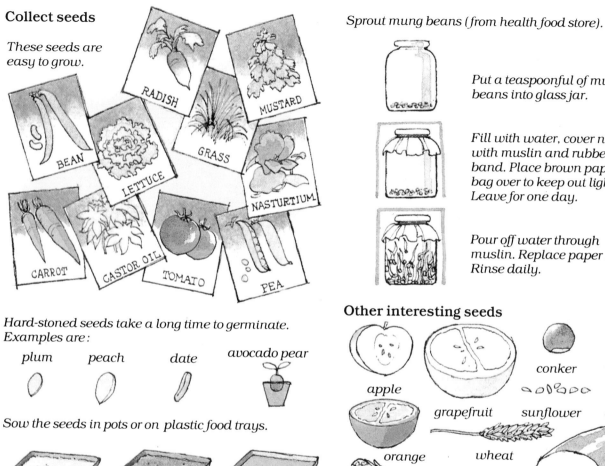

RADISH
MUSTARD
BEAN
GRASS
LETTUCE
NASTURTIUM
CARROT
CASTOR OIL
TOMATO
PEA

Hard-stoned seeds take a long time to germinate. Examples are:

plum   peach   date   *avocado pear*

Sow the seeds in pots or on plastic food trays.

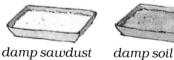

damp sawdust   damp soil   damp blotting paper

damp sand   damp cloth   damp paper towel

Keep lightly watered. Keep in the cool over a weekend. Sow in a pot, too.

tag

loamy potting compost

Sprout mung beans (from health food store).

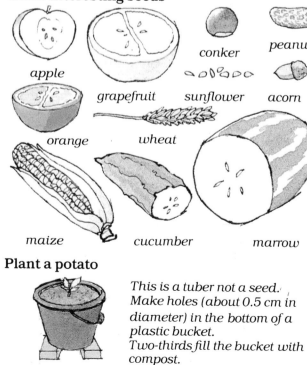

Put a teaspoonful of mung beans into glass jar.

Fill with water, cover neck with muslin and rubber band. Place brown paper bag over to keep out light. Leave for one day.

Pour off water through muslin. Replace paper bag. Rinse daily.

Other interesting seeds

apple   grapefruit   conker   peanut

orange   sunflower   acorn

wheat

maize   cucumber   marrow

Plant a potato

This is a tuber not a seed. Make holes (about 0.5 cm in diameter) in the bottom of a plastic bucket. Two-thirds fill the bucket with compost.

Grow in other ways

grass

painted egg shell

Trim the 'hair' with scissors.

Try a carrot top in a saucer of water. Try a parsnip and a swede, too.

Try an onion or a hyacinth bulb.

Fill the bottle with water.

Grow other things

offsets   leaf cuttings

soft tip cuttings

leaf incision (Begonia rex)

Make some bottle gardens

sweet jar

gravel and small stones underneath

potting compost and charcoal on top

kitchen storage jar

pickle jar

Use whatever large jars you can find around.

Make a garden in a box or a large flowerpot

Place it in the most effective spot.

Try a 'water garden'

large goldfish bowl

aquatic plants from garden centres

washed sand small stones

Try a washing-up bowl garden

sieved soil

Make a flower bed near a wall

Plant out window boxes

Make a garden in a sink

Try to find a ceramic sink.

margarine tub 'pool'

rockery plants

alyssum

stones

potting compost

Grow oak and sycamore seedlings in the sink.

Make a chequer-board garden

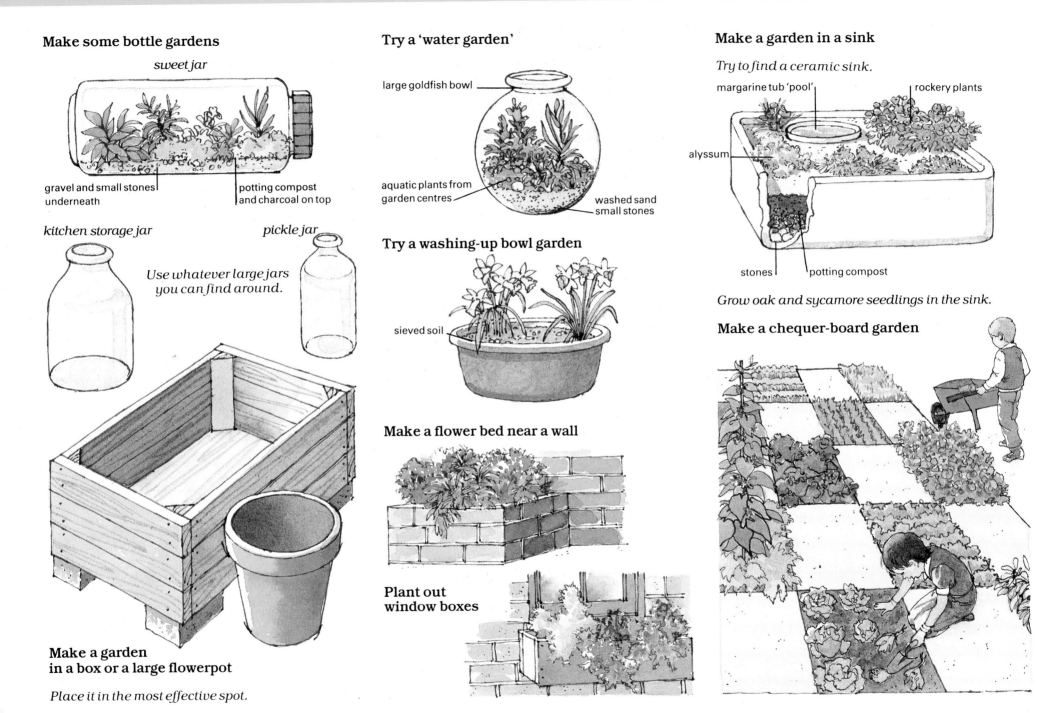

Make a miniature garden

Take a large metal tray and plan out your areas.

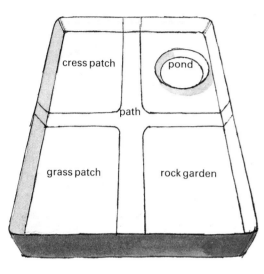

cress patch

pond

path

grass patch

rock garden

Use some ready-mixed sand and cement from a DIY shop to make your rockery and garden path.

SAND AND CEMENT

matchbox trays

Fill the boxes to make cement paving slabs.

Set out the rockery and paths.
Fill the areas for grass and cress with John Innes compost. Pat it down with a small brick.

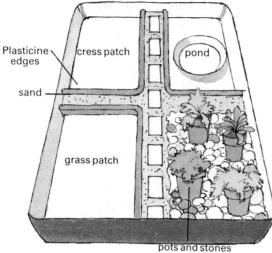

Plasticine edges

cress patch

pond

sand

grass patch

pots and stones embedded in cement

plant with mustard or cress in rows

pond

plant with grass seed

cement paving slabs embedded in sand

Water the garden very gently each day. Keep it in a cool place.

The finished garden

Trim the grass with scissors.

surround pond with gravel

If you like, you can put lights in your garden.

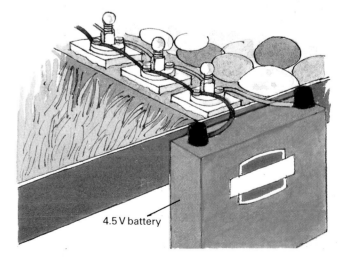

4.5 V battery

Primary colours

The primary colours of sunlight are red, green and blue.
They cannot be made by mixing other colours.

Secondary colours

Secondary colours are made by mixing red, green and blue:

red and green give yellow	*blue and green give cyan*
red and blue give magenta	*red, green and blue make white.*

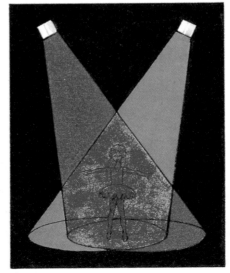
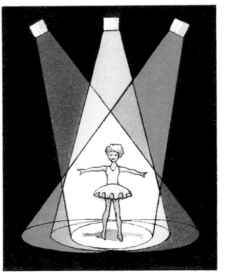

Reflected colours

Make a stage set. Shine on to the set a powerful torch covered in turn with different coloured tissue papers. What happens each time to the colours in the set?

See-through colours

Find some coloured containers to look through. What do other colours look like when viewed through the containers?

Make a display.

What is the colour of water in each coloured container?
Colour water with food dye. What does the solution look like in each coloured container?

Let children pretend they are visitors from outer space and can only see through red, blue or green. What effect does this have?

Seeing through red		
Things looked at	Colour seen	Colour it really is

Make some bold coloured pictures with powder paint or brightly coloured gummed paper.

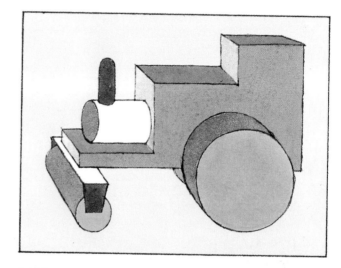

What do these look like viewed through different coloured pieces of acetate?

Mixing the primary colours

The primary colours of paint are different from those of light. They are yellow, red and blue.

More mixing

Mix some blue and some yellow paint.

Paint some of the new colour on paper as a record.

Add a little more of one colour.

Record the result on the same piece of paper.

Go on doing this. How many slightly different colours can you make?

Experiment with other pairs of colours. Try:
yellow and red
green and red
blue and red

Make shades of one colour

Mix some paint. Use pink or pale yellow.
Paint a small piece of paper. Write No 1 on the back.

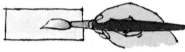

Add one tiny drop of black to the pink pot. Stir well.
Paint another piece of paper. Write No 2 on the back.

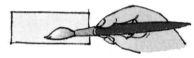

Add one more tiny drop of black. Stir well.
Paint another piece of paper. Write No 3 on the back.

Repeat this 20 times. You now have 20 shades of one colour.

Can children sort them in order?

Sorting out colours

*Can you sort the colours into
happy and sad colours
hot and cold colours
nasty and nice colours
summer and winter colours
young and old colours?*

*Make some paintings to represent some of these
colour groupings. For example, paint some happy
paintings and some sad paintings.*

Experiment with blobs of paint

Drop spots of paint on to wet paper. Tilt the paper.

*Place a blob of colour on paper. Blow it with a
straw.*

Blow gently, then blow hard.

Paste a sheet of paper.   *Drop on spots of paint.*

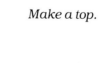

*Press on another sheet of
paper.*

Then peel apart.

Spin some colour

Make a whizzer.

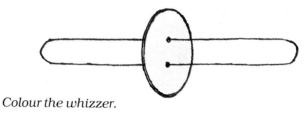

Colour the whizzer.

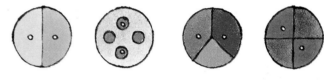

Spin the whizzer. What happens to the colours?

Make a top.

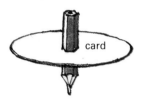
card

Colour the top.

*What happens when the top spins?
Red and green give…?
Blue and yellow give…?*

Colour travelling

Which colours stand out best?

Make up a test to find out.

Investigate how background colour affects the way in which we see the main colour being studied.

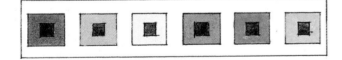

Try other background and other main colours.

Look for rainbows on a rainy day

Hold a glass prism up to the light.
Try a piece of old glass chandelier, too.

What happens when you move the prism or chandelier glass?

Put a bowl of water,
on which oil is floating,
in bright sunshine.

Experiment with coloured tissue paper

How does colour change when pieces are overlapped?
Try holding your picture up to the light.

Colour or things – which do you remember best?

Let children look at this picture for a minute. Take it away.
How many things can they remember?
How many colours of things can they remember?
Are some colours more easily remembered than others?
Keep a record of results to check.

If 15 things are too many for some children to try, cover up some of the picture and restrict the number of things shown at any one time.

Let children make their own charts to try on one another.

There are two important concepts to be considered:
the sequence of events
the duration of events
Here are some activities that will help develop an idea of the sequence of events.

Make a picture clock

A simple one for very young children.

A more complex one for children at a later stage of development.

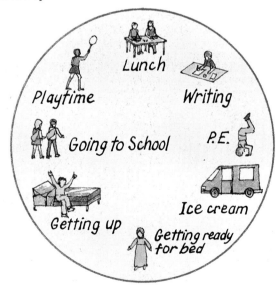

Make some picture cards

Getting up

Breakfast

Going to school

Assembly

Milk time

Lunch

Ask the children to put them in order.

Discuss what the children did yesterday, what they have done today, and what they are going to do tomorrow.

Words to develop are: before
after
yesterday
today
tomorrow
night
day

Make a chart of the day's events in the correct order

Susie's day

Painting

In the home bay

Worked with the abacus

Lunch

Planted seeds

Story time

Make a chart of the week's events showing special happenings

Monday – Jill brought her rabbit

Tuesday – Carol's birthday

Wednesday – PC Rose visited

Thursday – Fire drill

Friday – Class took assembly

Here are some activities that will help develop the concept of the duration of events, and some ideas for making 'clocks' to time those events.

Water clocks

Plasticine with pin-hole right through

hole to let in air

plastic bowl weighted with Plasticine

small hole

How many blocks can you put in line before the water clock sinks?

Sand clock

Candle clocks

One candle can be marked against the burning of another, e.g. at 5 minute intervals.

How many things can you do whilst a birthday candle burns through?

Does it matter where you put the candles?

Some activities

Whilst the timer empties:

How far can you hop?

How many bounces of the ball?

How many times can you run round skittles in the playground?

How many marbles can you put in the pot – one at a time?

How many times can you write your whole name?

The following experiences will help children eventually to understand that:
The sun is a source of light.
The sharpness of shadows will vary with different weather conditions.
The angle at which light falls on an object will affect the shape of the shadow.
Time can be told from the positions of shadows.
By observing the changing positions of shadows, one can gauge the relative movement of the earth and the sun.

Look at shadows at different times of the day

When are they long? When are they short?
When are they sharp? When are they fuzzy?

How can you get thin shadows? How can you get fat shadows?

Shake hands and watch your shadows shake hands

Can you enclose an object in a shadow cast by your arms?

Can you hide your shadow?

Make a shadow play

Now it's a circle!

Can you get your shadows to shake hands without touching your own hands together?

Make a shadow with six arms

Now it's an eight!

Can you stand on each other's heads?

Draw round a shadow

Make some shadows on the wall

Draw round a shadow on sugar paper and cut it out

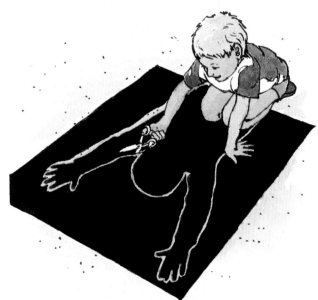

Draw a shadow through the day

Use a shadow stick to mark the sun's passage

Collect shells

Look at shells

Feel the insides and outsides.

Look at and draw the different openings.

Find spiral patterns. Where else can this pattern be found? (Screws, plants, records, staircase.) Are they all in the same direction?

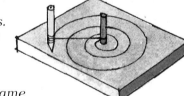

Draw a spiral.

How strong is a shell?

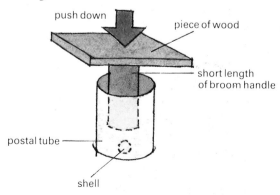

push down

piece of wood

short length of broom handle

postal tube

shell

Sort and compare

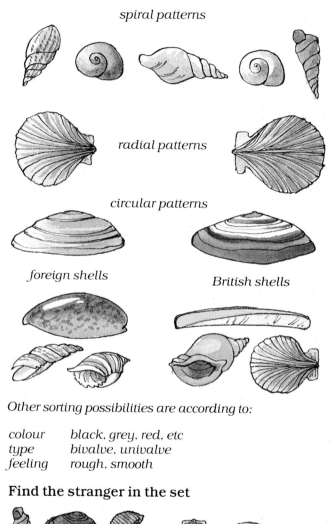

spiral patterns

radial patterns

circular patterns

foreign shells

British shells

Other sorting possibilities are according to:

colour	black, grey, red, etc
type	bivalve, univalve
feeling	rough, smooth

Find the stranger in the set

a land shell among sea shells

a smooth shell among rough shells

Collect stones and pebbles

Sort and compare

layered structure

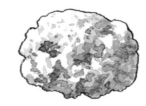

pudding-like structure

rounded   *jagged*

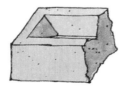

artificial   *natural*

patterned   *plain*

Which is the heaviest?

Feel the heaviness of each stone.

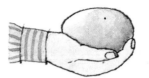

Put them in order. Check by using scales.

Pebbles are rounded and formed by rubbing and wear. Look for other examples of rubbing and rounding. Compare the following with their original shape.

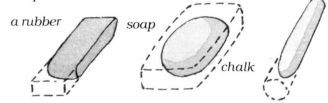

a rubber   *soap*

chalk

Make a pebble from clay

Discuss how a pebble was really made. Then make a 'holed' pebble. How was a hole really made?

Make some 'stone'

sand   *small stones*   *cement*   *water*

Mix these together. Mould the mixture in a matchbox. Turn out when dry.

Collect bricks and blocks

These help to develop ideas of form, pattern and space as well as mathematical relationships.

Hestair Hope's
Jumbo Bag

Plastibrics

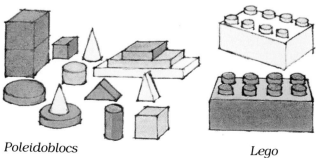

wood bricks

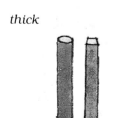

Poleidoblocs

Lego

Sorting by material

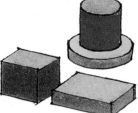

plastic

wood

clay (real bricks)

Sorting by size

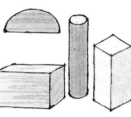

small

large

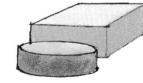

thick

thin

tall

short

Sorting by colour

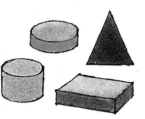

red

blue

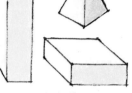

green

yellow

Sorting by shape

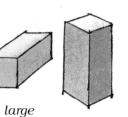

cube

cuboid

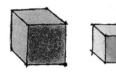

triangular prism

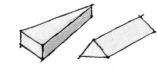

pyramid

cylinder

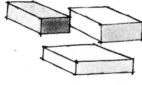

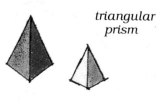

Collect seeds

Get different kinds and sizes.

coconut

grass seeds

cactus seeds

sunflower

wheat, maize, barley, oats

tree seeds

peas

beans

vegetable seeds

wild flower seeds

ornamental gourd seeds

Sort seeds in their cases

Fleshy structures

grapes

plum

tomato

apple

melon

marrow

Dry cases

lupin

beech

acorn

poppy

pea

chestnut

Sort and compare

Talk about different sizes of seed. Feel the varying textures. Look at the colours. Discuss the different shapes. Make patterns by sorting the seeds according to

colour

large and small

rough and smooth

Then make a picture.

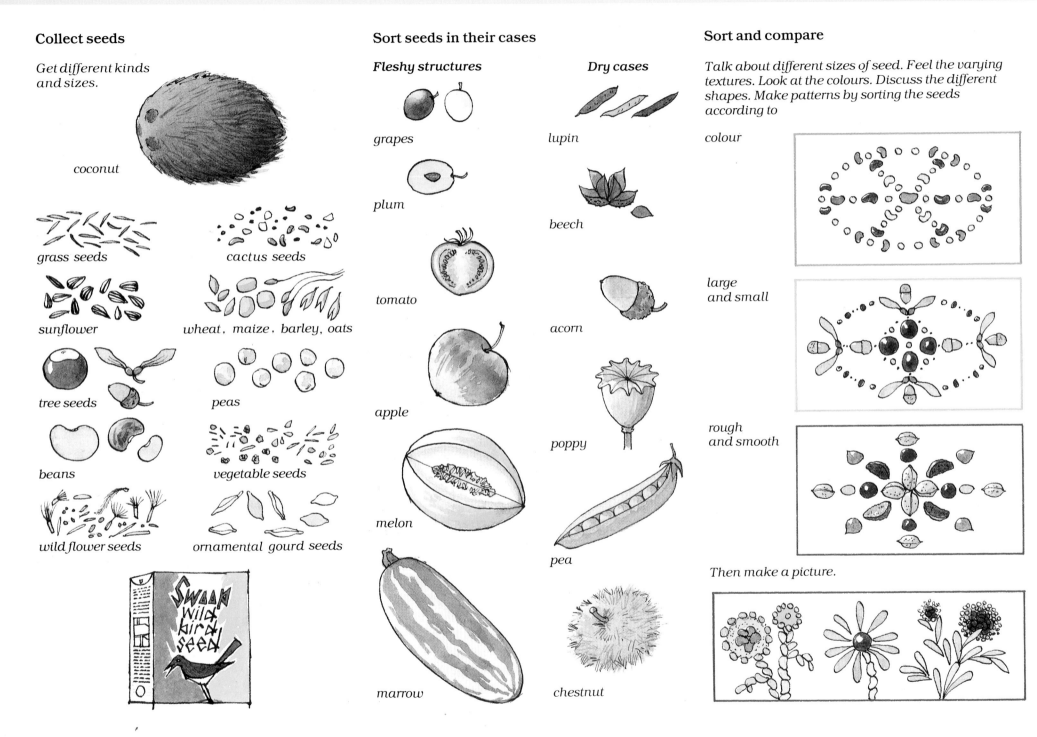

Measuring seeds

Which is the largest we can find?
Which is the smallest?

How many can you lay into a 2 cm square?
Try each of the following:

sunflower
pea
bean
wheat

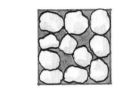

How many peas or beans does it take to fill an eggcup?

Soaking seeds

Seeds need water to grow. What happens when we soak them? Use peas. Do they get bigger when they are soaked?

Measure their size when they are dry and when wet. Compare the two sets of measurements. How heavy are the peas when dry and when wet?

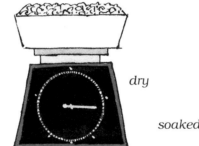

dry

soaked

Soaked seeds are easier to take apart and study. Soak some peas, beans, maize. Use cocktail sticks to take them apart.

Planting and growing

What containers can we grow seeds in?

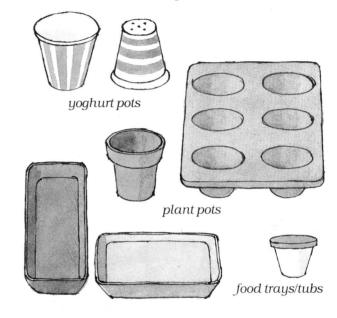

yoghurt pots

plant pots

food trays/tubs

What base can we grow the seeds in? Try each of the following:

garden soil   *sand*   *sawdust*

JOHN INNES Seed compost

cotton wool

VERMICULITE

How shall we plant them?
One rule is to cover the seeds with a layer of soil the same size as the seeds.
Another is to read the instructions on the packet!
Try sowing the seeds at different depths. What happens? What do they need to make them grow?

Fasteners on us

Make a survey.

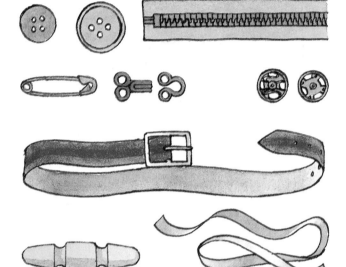

Talk about ways of fastening clothes.

Other fastener activities

Get the children to sort their shoes into groups.

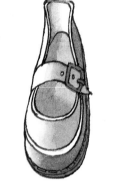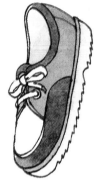

Which group has most?

Look for the use of elastic in dresses, trousers, blouses, tops, knickers, pants, socks. Investigate the stretch.

Have a 'fastening-up-coats' race

Count the number of buttons on your garments

Who has most? Who has least?

Elroy	Joan	Liz
12	3	6

Collect and sort buttons

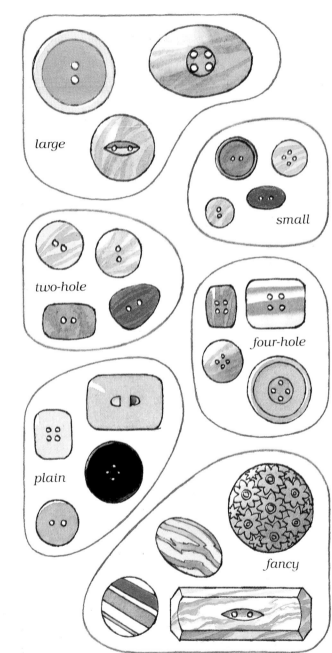

large

small

two-hole

four-hole

plain

fancy

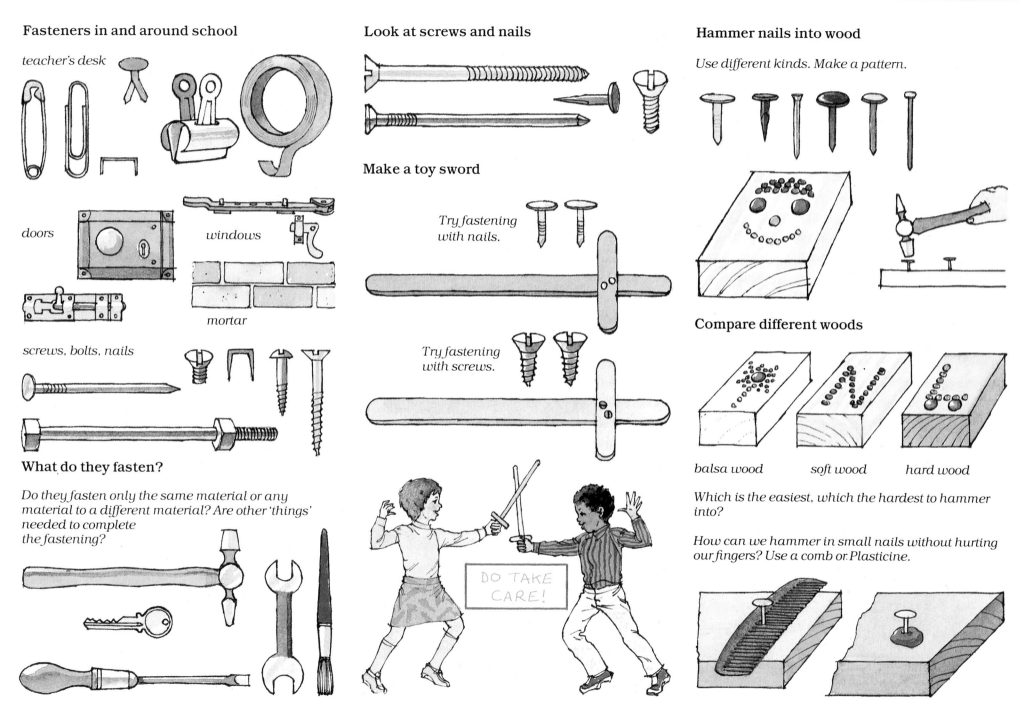

Fasteners in and around school

teacher's desk

doors

windows

mortar

screws, bolts, nails

What do they fasten?

Do they fasten only the same material or any material to a different material? Are other 'things' needed to complete the fastening?

Look at screws and nails

Make a toy sword

Try fastening with nails.

Try fastening with screws.

DO TAKE CARE!

Hammer nails into wood

Use different kinds. Make a pattern.

Compare different woods

balsa wood   *soft wood*   *hard wood*

Which is the easiest, which the hardest to hammer into?

How can we hammer in small nails without hurting our fingers? Use a comb or Plasticine.

Collect bottles and jars

Sort and compare

What did the bottles originally contain? Was it, for example:

food
drink
medicine
ink
perfume?

Are there any links between the colour of a bottle and its use?
Which is the tallest, which the smallest?
Which holds the most, which the least?

Sort and compare the kinds of stopper used.

screw on   plastic   cork

Filling and emptying

Seal in one funnel with Plasticine. What happens?

Use the smallest bottle to fill the largest. How many times will it take? Guess, then try.

Tie a piece of muslin over the top of a filled bottle. Turn it upside down to empty. What happens? Turn it sideways to empty. What happens?

Use bottles of the same size. Fill with varying amounts of water.

Tap each. Listen. Blow over each. Listen

Symmetrical bottles

These bottles are symmetrical. Are all bottles symmetrical?

Cut out some symmetrical bottle shapes from card. Place these shapes on tissue paper, and draw around them. Cut out the tissue paper shapes. Overlap the tissue paper bottles in a pattern.

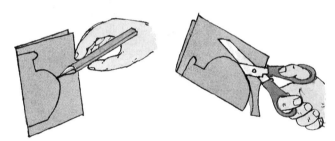

Other things to do

Fill a small bottle with water.

Seal it.

Hold the bottle just above some print. What do you see?

Messages have been sent across the sea in bottles. When will a bottle stay afloat? When will it sink?

Is the bottle empty? Push it under water. What happens?

Are all bottles stable?

Fill a jar with a screw-on lid. Knock a hole in the lid.

Turn upside down to empty. Try two holes.

Make a bottle garden.

Collect toy animals

farmyard animals

wooden zoo animals

Noah's Ark with animals

Visit farms and wildlife parks

Sort and compare

farm animals

wild animals

animals with hair

pets

animals from hot lands

animals with feathers

animals from our country

animals from cold lands

animals with scales

animals which hunt

animals seen in zoos

animals which are hunted

animals from far-off lands

Look at hunted animals

Notice their long legs
large ears
eyes at side of head.

Why are they like this?

Do large ears help?

Make a 'big ear'. Cut out this shape from a sheet of cartridge paper and roll it into a cone.

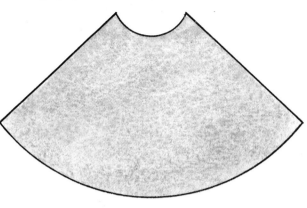

Tape the edges together.

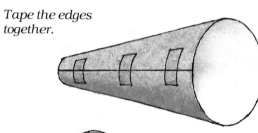

Test it.
Make a tiny sound.
Listen without the 'big ear'.
Listen with the 'big ear'.

What about spots and stripes?

Some animals are striped.
Some are spotted.
Some are coloured and patterned.
They use colour and pattern to hide from their enemies.

Paint a background against which you can 'hide' your animal. Try out how well the animal is hidden against the background.

Paint a scrap card box and 'hide' it against a background.

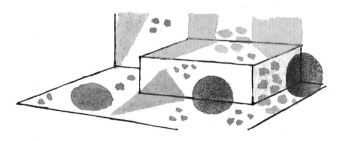

In schools where classrooms are very small and overcrowded, experience with water may have to be provided out of doors in summer time.

In winter children should use lukewarm water.

The plastic pond

The cloakroom sink

The water tank

Looking after resources

It is possible to collect many more small pieces of equipment than children can use with water at any one time. If these are grouped in boxes, according to the type of experience they offer, each set can be exploited in turn, while the other boxes remain in the school resources bank or are used by other classes. Notes about ways of using the contents of each box and of talking about them can be written on each lid.

Hot or cold?

Get the children to put one hand in very warm water and the other hand in cold water. Then get them to put both hands in lukewarm water.

Does the water in the middle basin feel lukewarm to both hands?

very warm
water

cold water

lukewarm water

Pushing it about

Water in a plastic bag can be pushed about and squeezed. Could we use this as a cushion?

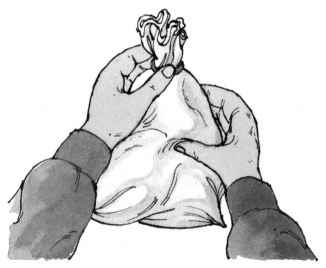

Drops, streams and jets

Let the children feel drops, streams and jets of water falling from different heights. How can they be described?

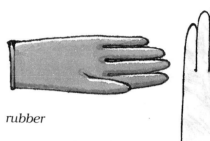

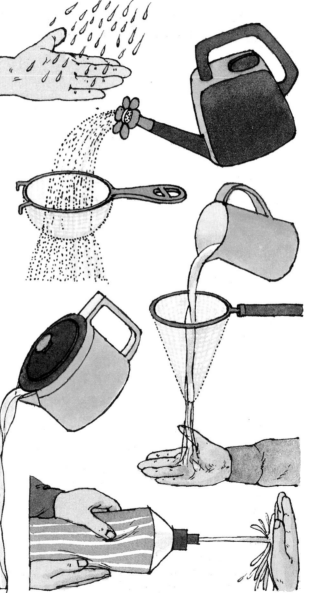

Using gloves

Can we feel water with gloves on? Does any type of glove prevent us from feeling water? Does water roll off or soak into any of these gloves?

rubber

kid   nylon

woolly mitten

Can we wring the water out of any gloves?

Squeezing wet things

Can we get water out of things by squeezing them? Try the following:

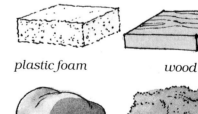

plastic foam   wood

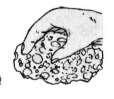

bath sponge

clay   felt, blanket
or flannel

Moving things in water

Here are some things we can move to and fro in water:

our own hands with fingers
apart and fingers together

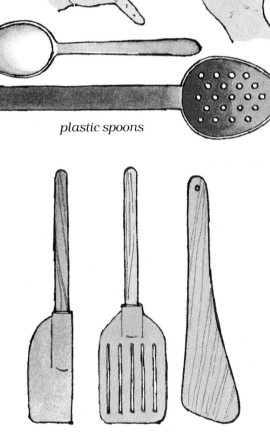

plastic spoons

kitchen spatulas
with blades of
rubber, wood or plastic

What else makes a good paddle?
Is it better to swim with open or closed fingers?
Why do ducks have webbed feet?
How do flippers help you to swim?
Do they help you to walk on land?
Who can draw the oar of a boat?
Do you have to push harder when you walk through a deep puddle in your wellingtons?

Let children feel still and moving water.
Use a whisk to make water move. Vary the speed of the whisk. What happens?

Words

For conversation about activities.
To look up in picture dictionaries.
To add to a list on the classroom wall.

hot	splashes
cold	knocks
warm	hits
lukewarm	wring
wet	squeeze
smooth	shake
slippery	sponge
transparent	wood
hard	clay
soft	flannel
bounces	fingers
drops	spoons
trickle	pushers
stream	whisk
jet	moving
plops	still
force	waves

passes through (permeable)
rolls off (impermeable)
soaks in (absorbed)
falls downward

Children can:
talk
add to their own word books
draw pictures
add captions to pictures

Ideas children can meet

The fluidity and transparency of water.
The feel of variations in temperature.
The force with which water can strike.
The greater the distance through which water falls, the harder it strikes (i.e. the greater force it exerts).
The resistance water offers to the different kinds of surfaces being pushed against it.
Water can pass through or soak into some materials but not others.

Take two similar pieces of material. Make one wet.
Keep the other dry.
Move the wet material to a dry place.
What happens?

Try with

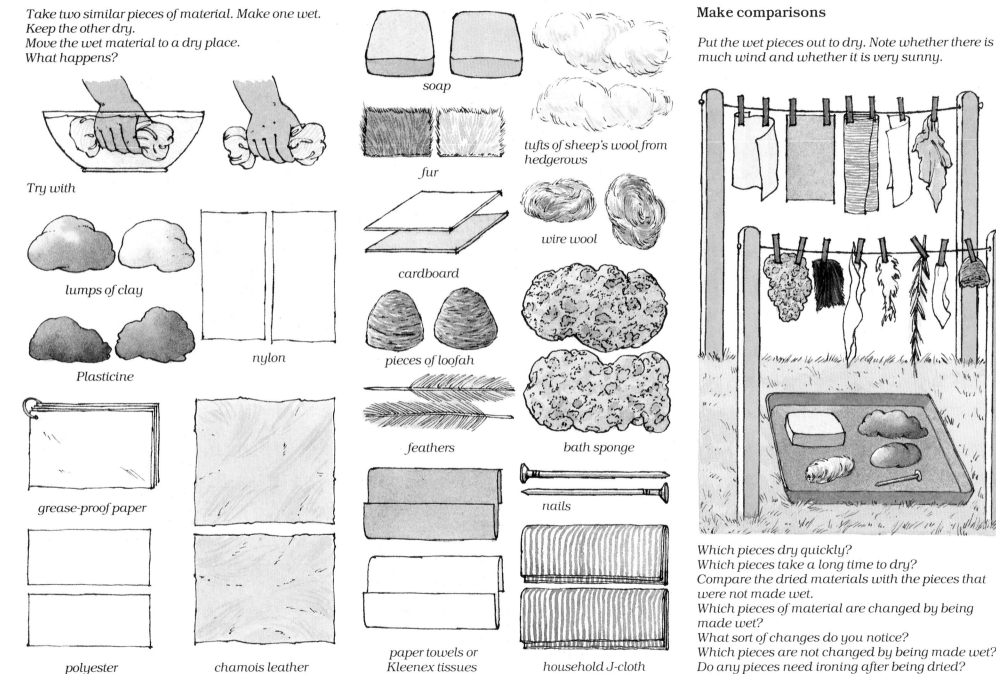

lumps of clay

Plasticine

nylon

grease-proof paper

polyester

chamois leather

soap

fur

tufts of sheep's wool from hedgerows

cardboard

wire wool

pieces of loofah

feathers

bath sponge

nails

paper towels or
Kleenex tissues

household J-cloth

Make comparisons

Put the wet pieces out to dry. Note whether there is much wind and whether it is very sunny.

Which pieces dry quickly?
Which pieces take a long time to dry?
Compare the dried materials with the pieces that were not made wet.
Which pieces of material are changed by being made wet?
What sort of changes do you notice?
Which pieces are not changed by being made wet?
Do any pieces need ironing after being dried?

Damp places

What happens to things left in damp places?

orange peel

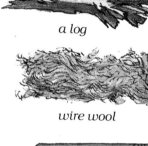

a log

wire wool

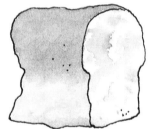

a piece of bread

a painted nail and an unpainted nail

Drying up

What happens to puddles in the playground when it stops raining?

What happens to different soils as they dry? Look at

peat   clay   loam   sand

Put some water in a shallow plate on the classroom window sill. Watch the water level every day.

Hang some wet pieces of J-cloth in warm, cold, windy and still places. How long do they take to dry? Why must each piece be equally wet and the same size?

Words and records

Wet and Dry things	Made wet	Dry again
Paper towel	can be squeezed into a soggy ball	a hard ball
Grease-proof paper	bends over will not rattle	stiff rattles again
Clay	soft; sticky	hard
Chamois leather	slimy	stiff
Soap	a slippery lump	a smooth lump

Ideas children can meet

Things in damp places can rot and break up or become mouldy or get rusty.
Paint prevents metal things from rusting.
Mouldy things in a classroom need care and supervision. Keep them covered.

Drying J-Cloth	
Place	Time
On line in a windy garden	10 minutes
Against radiator	5 minutes

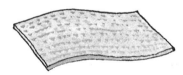

Paint and creosote on wood prevent it from rotting.
Materials with different properties are affected by water in different ways.
We can change some things by making them wet and then drying them.
Some things are changed permanently by being made wet. Others change temporarily when they are made wet, then allowed to dry.
When making a test, a control is needed. This is an identical piece of material which is not given the test treatment.

Useful concepts are:
absorbing (soaking up)
rusting
rotting
evaporation (drying up)

What shall we use?

Provide a choice of containers. Test their suitability by standing them out in the rain in the same place for the same length of time.

How shall we measure rainfall?

Measure the depth of water in the container (the rain gauge). The container chosen must have straight sides. Reject vessels that are easily blown over, too small, have narrow necks or are too open and allow evaporation.

Where shall we put our rain gauge?

Place a number of similar containers on open ground, in places where rain can drip into them from other surfaces, and in sheltered places.

Comparing amounts of rain

At this stage, it is enough to help children to find out that more rain falls on some days than on others. For this, measuring tubes are useful.

Label the tubes according to the days of the week. Place squared paper on a screen behind the tubes. Pour the water collected in the rain gauge into the relevant tube. Make a bar chart on squared paper showing the amount of rain collected each day.

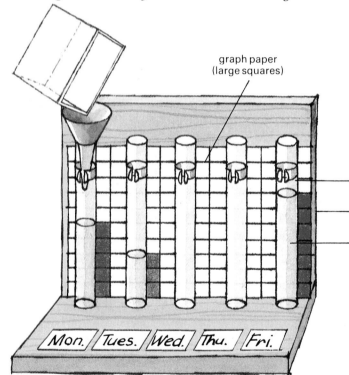

graph paper
(large squares)

Terry clip

wooden stand

Alka Seltzer tube

Mon. | Tues. | Wed. | Thu. | Fri.

Mount a collection of these records in a book, like the one shown on the far right.

Do the records show any patterns? For example:
the wettest week of the month
the driest week of the month
the month with most rain
the weeks with no rain.

Improving the rain gauge

In the light of our experience of drying (evaporation) (see page 45), we need an improved rain gauge which lets the rain in, while also preventing evaporation.

Cut the top from a squeezy bottle, invert it and push it down into the remaining part of the bottle. Set the gauge firmly in the ground.

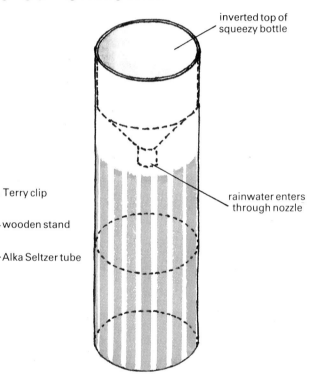

inverted top of
squeezy bottle

rainwater enters
through nozzle

When will it be best to empty the rain gauge? (The same time each day.)

Perhaps some children would like to make their own gauge. They could then keep records at home over the weekends.

Some children may be able to compare their measurements with published rainfall figures.

Words and records

wet	dripping	funnel
drop	spreading	jar
drizzle	wettest	bottle
shower	driest	tin
downpour	more	plate
rain	less	dish
snow	most	small
dew	least	big
hail	same	deep
heavy	full	shallow
light	empty	straight
falling	overflowing	rain gauge
downward	evaporation	

This year may not be like other years. Keep this book of records to compare with those made in other years.

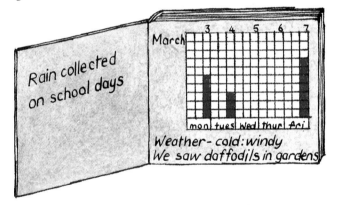

Rain collected on school days

March

mon | tues | wed | thur | Fri

Weather - cold: windy
We saw daffodils in gardens

Ideas children can meet

Water spreads and flows if not contained.
Rainfall can be measured by recording the depth of rain collected.
The width and depth of water changes when transferred from the rain gauge to the measuring tubes, but the total amount of water remains unchanged – an example of conservation of volume.
Information can be presented in a number of different graphical ways.

Look at raindrops falling on the classroom window

What size are they? How do they move, meet, separate? Is the rain falling in a shower or a downpour?

Isolate single drops

Single drops of water can be isolated using various things:

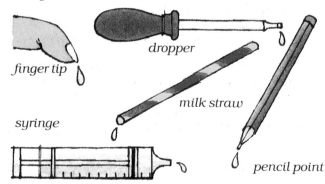

dropper

finger tip

milk straw

syringe

pencil point

Look at a drop on a surface

Look at a drop's shape. Then look through it. What do you notice?

What happens to a drop of water when placed on different surfaces? Try:

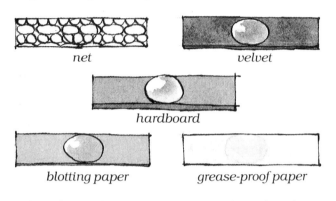

net   velvet

hardboard

blotting paper   grease-proof paper

Place drops of water on some printed words. What happens to the print?

a picture for y**O**to colour

What happens when sunlight falls on drops of water?

Make ripples on the surface of a bowl of water using a dropper.

Look on the surface of the water for reflections.

Look at ice cubes

Can you see through an ice cube? Does it smell?

Drop an ice cube into a glass of water. What do you notice?

Put in a pencil. What do you notice?

Smelling water – and safety training

This activity needs to be carefully controlled as indiscriminate smelling can be dangerous. Emphasize that things such as plant sprays, insect sprays and certain household chemicals may be poisonous. Unknown things must not be smelt without a teacher's or parent's consent.

Whenever the opportunity arises, draw children's attention to smells connected with water. Some examples are the fresh smell brought by rain after a dry spell, the smell of damp places, the smell of damp clothes in a school cloakroom and the unpleasant smell of stagnant, polluted water (remind them this can be a warning of danger). Provide safe liquids for children to distinguish from water by smelling, for example:

More safety training

This is another activity needing control because of hygiene and the hazards of poisons. Make sure the children use individual spoons, cups or straws. Foods for tasting must be fresh. Never taste unknown things without a teacher's consent.

Distinguish by tasting

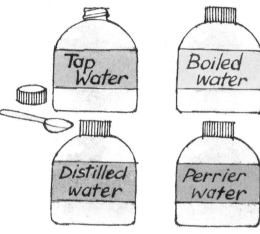

Things that change the taste of water are:

Other things to taste and compare with water are:

grapefruit (bitter)

Oxo cube (salty)

acid drop   *sweets and fruit flavours*

Weak and strong flavours

Compare the flavour when different amounts of sugar are added to tap water.

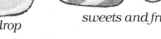

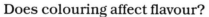

Does colouring affect flavour?

Taste water to which different food colouring materials have been added.

Words and records

Looking

small	waves	magnify
large	ice	bigger
round	permeable	smaller
flat	impermeable	glitter
long	slow	rainbow
solid	coalesce	circle
liquid	drop	white
fast	stream	crooked
transparent	trickle	split
shining	spread	
ripples	soak	
reflections	absorbent	

Smelling

fresh	mouldy	colourless
damp	pleasant	stink
clean	unpleasant	sniff
dirty	scent	

Tasting

fizzy	sour	acid
sweet	bitter	nice
strong	weak	nasty

Children can talk, add to word books, write freely in news books and draw pictures about their experiences of looking, smelling and tasting water.

Ideas children can meet

The different amounts of water that fall in a shower and a downpour.
Rain can fall continuously throughout the day or intermittently in showers or sudden cloudbursts.
The different amounts of force experienced from a drop, a stream or jet of water.
The 'magnifying glass' effect of a drop of water.
The differences between solids and liquids.
Not all colourless liquids are water.
The strengths of flavours are weakened by dilution.

What spreads?

What things spread when they are poured from containers? How do they spread? Do they pile up?

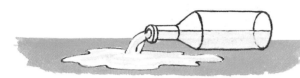

Where do puddles collect after rain?

Look for hollows in the ground.

Collect containers for making water into different shapes

Small shampoo and bath salt containers are very suitable.

Filling

The problem of filling bottles with narrow necks can be solved by using a funnel.

What else changes shape?

Other materials that can take the shape of their containers are sand, sugar and dry silt. Magnify these materials. Note that individual particles keep their own shapes.

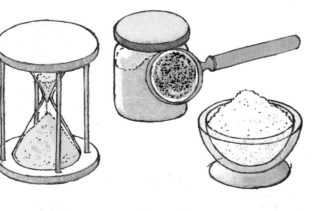

Moving water in different ways

Another way in which children can meet the idea of water taking the shape of its container is to use plastic funnels and tubing. Vary the sizes of the funnels, the diameter and length of the tubing and the quantities of water used. Link with work on the measurement of time.

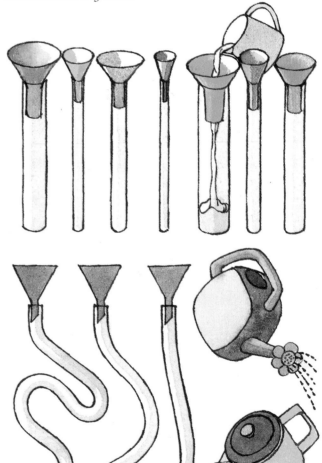

Make a pouring cup from a squeezy bottle.

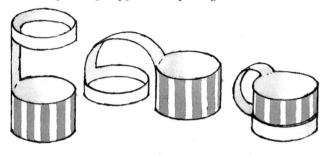

How can we move water from B to A without adding any from the tap?

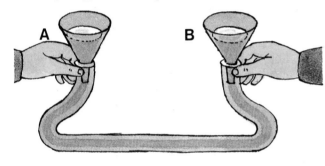

Make interesting routes for water by joining plastic bottles and tubing together.

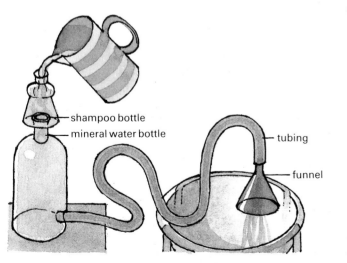

shampoo bottle
mineral water bottle
tubing
funnel

Pour water into a squeezy bottle in which holes have been made at different heights.
Keep the holes covered until the bottle is full. What do you notice when the holes are uncovered?

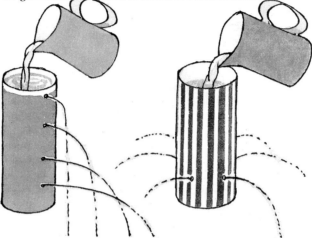

Make a water clock.

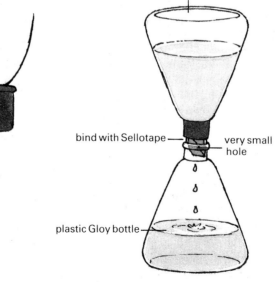

cut away base

bind with Sellotape
very small hole

plastic Gloy bottle

Try using other liquids such as detergent, milk and treacle.
Is there any difference when these are used?

Words and records

puddle	full
hollow	empty
shapeless	bottle
irregular	gun
spill	boot
flow	Dalek
spread	engine
flat	funnel
thin	narrow
long	wide
short	liquid
tall	solid

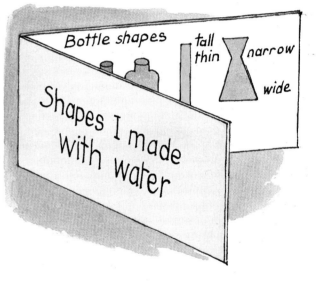

Bottle shapes
tall
thin
narrow
wide
Shapes I made with water

Ideas children can meet

The difference between liquids and solids.
Fluidity – a liquid spreads and flows unless it is contained.
Water takes the shape of the vessel it occupies or of the space it passes through.
Solids keep their shape unless damaged.
Materials consisting of small separate particles can be poured into containers of different shapes. The separate particles keep their own shapes. Try pouring silver sand and table salt.

Home-made cups

Five or six containers cut from the bases of plastic bottles. They should be cut to the same depth in order to hold equal amounts of water.

How much will a cup hold?

empty   *full*   *overflowing*

Different shapes – same volume

Measuring the size (volume) of awkward shapes

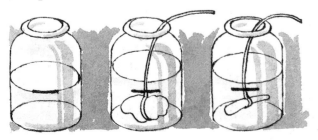

Containers for measuring different quantities

Kitchen equipment is often useful.

feeding bottles   kitchen jugs   plastic spoons

measuring spoon – push 'piston' to give required amount

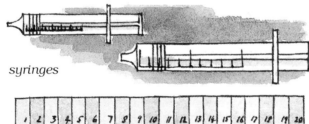

syringes

| 1 | 2 | 3 | 4 | 5 | 6 | 7 | 8 | 9 | 10 | 11 | 12 | 13 | 14 | 15 | 16 | 17 | 18 | 19 | 20 |

rulers

Containers marked in fractional quantities

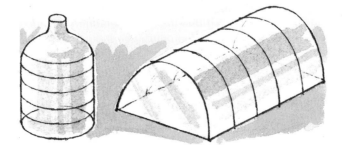

Bottles holding different quantities

Arrange the bottles in order of the amounts they can hold when filled.

Litre analysis bottles

These are a set of 17 plastic bottles to give children experience with metric volumes. The set consists of:

$10 \times 100 \ cm^3$
$4 \times 250 \ cm^3$
$2 \times 500 \ cm^3$
$1 \times 1000 \ cm^3$

Polypropylene jugs

Such a jug has moulded graduations, a spout and handle. It is almost transparent and is resistant to acids, alkalis and organic solvents. The jug comes in the following volumes: 500, 1000 and 2000 cm^3, graduations of 50, 50 and 100 cm^3 respectively.

Newton meters

These are useful for weighing things in and out of water.

Measuring jugs

These are usually supplied as a set of four. They are made from high-quality transparent plastic which is slightly flexible and not brittle. The calibrations are easy to read. The set comprises one each of 2000 cm^3 calibrated every 250 cm^3, 1000 cm^3 calibrated every 100 cm^3, 500 cm^3 and 250 cm^3 calibrated every 50 cm^3.

Always take readings at eye-level.

Litre set

This is a set of four transparent plastic containers, each with a capacity of 1 litre. Actually, each is just over a litre and has a mark near the rim which indicates the height to which it must be filled to contain exactly 1 litre. The set comprises a cube, a rectangular box and two cylinders of different diameters.

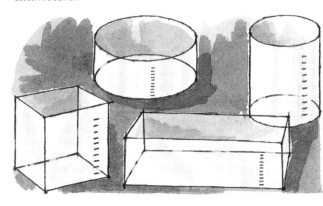

Litre cube

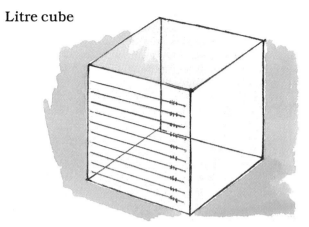

This is a transparent plastic cube of 1 litre capacity, one side of which has lines drawn across the face to represent volumes of from 100 cm^3 to 1000 cm^3 in steps of 100 cm^3.

Words and records

full	*large*	*falls*
empty	*transparent*	*irregular*
half	*colourless*	*quantity*
quarter	*equal*	*heavy*
three-quarters	*part*	*light*
over flowing	*first*	
more	*second*	
less	*most*	
similar	*least*	
small	*rises*	

Ideas children can meet

Depth
Width
Volume
Conservation of volume
Much
Little
Full
Empty
½, ¼, ⅓, ¾, full
Transparency
Series – from little to much

How hard do you have to push or squeeze to force water from these vessels?
How far can you make the water travel?

Indoor work

Use the pump to get water out of the bottle.

Get your syringe half full.

How can you pick up water with syringes, droppers and the meat baster?

Use the syphon to move water from the aquarium to a bowl.

WASHING UP LIQUID

Outdoor work

Watch the path of the squirted water.
Does a hard squeeze give a different path
from that of a soft squeeze?
What happens when a jet of water hits
a wall?
Squirt water at your friend's hands.
Can you make jets that hit with different
amounts of force?

Words

pull	gently	jet
push	squirt	stream
squeeze	near	trickle
hard	far	drops

Ideas children can meet

The concept of force.
Ways of exerting force by pushing, pulling and
squeezing.
The harder the push or squeeze (i.e. the greater the
force exerted), the further a thing travels if nothing
interferes with it.

Sort objects according to whether they float or sink in water

pumice

pebbles

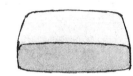

balls of different materials and sizes

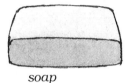

soap

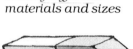

eraser

corks

bottle tops

metal things

Different kinds of water

What floats on ponds and rivers and what floats on the sea?
What happens when you put an egg and a block of wood into tap water and salty water?

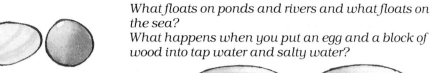

tap water   salty water

Does all wood float?

Try cubes of different types of wood, for example:

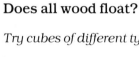

ash   pine   beech   oak

chestnut   elm   ebony   balsa

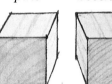

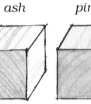
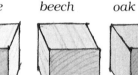

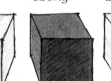

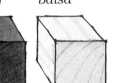

What else floats?

Can you go to sea in a sieve?
Provide a boat made of perforated zinc. (Bind the sharp edges.) Will it float?

Make a milk straw float upright by attaching paper clips to its base. How many paper clips are needed in different liquids to make the straw float?

Does a milk bottle top float or sink?

Make some boats

How well do they travel down a stream?
Make different boat shapes using the same amount of wood or polystyrene for each boat.
Make some with sails and some without. Try placing the sails in different positions.
Measure the time the boats take to travel the same distance.

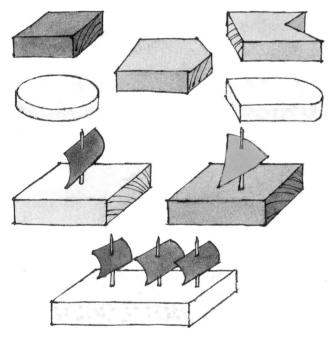

How much of an iceberg is under the water's surface?

Float an ice cube in both fresh and salty water to find out.

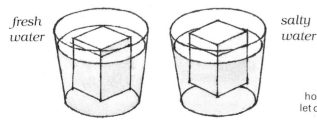

fresh water

salty water

What happens in water?

Try to push a block of polystyrene under water. What pushes the other way?

Attach a rubber band to a brick. Hold the brick up in the air. Hold it up in water. Notice the length of the rubber band each time.

Make a submarine by submerging a tin can or plastic bottle in water. Raise the submarine by forcing out the water it contains with air.

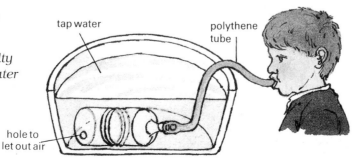

tap water

polythene tube

hole to let out air

Words and records

water	salty water	oval
heavy	boats	iceberg
light	sails	push
float	sieve	stretch
sink	square	rubber band
pebbles	oblong	tin
corks	wood	lid
balls	polystyrene	metal
blow	soap	spoon
air	rubber	fork
above	deep	knife
below	shallow	

Things in water	
Float	Sink

Get the children to make books for the class library.

Icebergs

How I raised a submarine

Boats on the stream

Ideas children can meet

Small, heavy objects can sink.
Large, light objects can float.
Differences in density.
Objects float more easily in some liquids than in others.
Buoyancy
Surface tension. (Even certain perforated objects can float on the surface of water.)
Objects containing air are often less dense and therefore lighter than the same volume of water.

Add things to cold and warm water

What happens? Does stirring help?

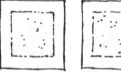
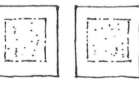

coffee bags

tea bags

*Did any substances not disappear in water?
Will they disappear in other liquids?
Do they change when they do not disappear?
Do they change the water?*

What does water do to jelly cubes?

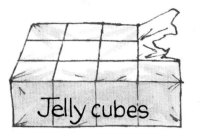

Can we get more lather?

If we use more and more soap flakes or washing-up liquid in water, do we get more lather? Do soap flakes help on wash day?

Make some soap films.

Who can blow the biggest bubble?

What happens to a coloured drop in water?

food colours

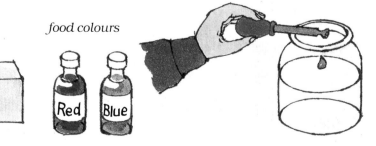

Can we extract things dissolved in water?

Find a hollow place where a puddle has been. Has anything been left behind in the hollow? Is there anything to feel?

Look inside the kettle. What may be left inside after the water has boiled away?

Make some clean water

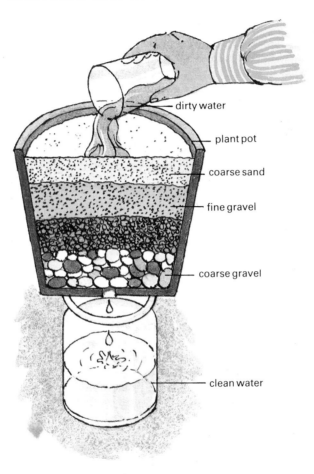

- dirty water
- plant pot
- coarse sand
- fine gravel
- coarse gravel
- clean water

Words and records

disappear	sugar	jelly cubes
dissolve	salt	arrowroot
stir	starch	tooth-paste
shake	soap-flakes	silt
insoluble	tea	kettle-fur
lather	coffee	filter
bubbles	cocoa	clean
soap film	flour	dirty
drying-up	dried milk	sand
evaporate	gelatine	gravel

Things in water	
soluble	insoluble
salt white sugar brown sugar	sand

Make some books for the class library.

Ideas children can meet

Solubility
Dilution
Soap films
The connection between the rate of dissolving and the temperature of the water.
Water can change materials.
Materials can change water.

Where can we find water in our neighbourhood?

puddles in the playground

fountains and ponds

gutters and water butt

Is the water *deep* or *shallow*?

Is it *moving*?

How much? Try a game of Pooh-sticks. The test must be fair.

Where can we find *much* water? Where can we find only a *little*?

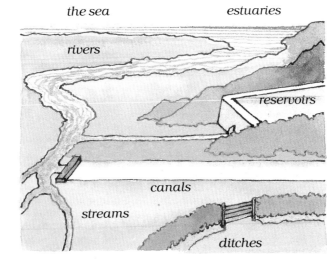

the sea   *estuaries*

rivers

reservoirs

canals

streams

ditches

What dries up quickly after rain?

Set up an observation using the following materials:

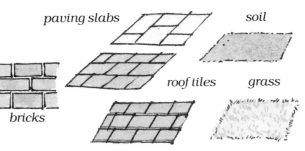

paving slabs   *soil*

roof tiles   *grass*

bricks

Feel water from a drizzle, a shower and a downpour

What kinds of cloud do we see on rainy days?

feathery white   *white, fat and puffy*

smooth and grey   *black and menacing*

Use your cloud reflector for collecting records. When do we see rainbows in the sky? Search for rainbows elsewhere.

How quickly does the washing dry in the garden?

Test the same garments on the following sorts of days: sunny, dull, still and breezy. Begin with them equally wet. How can we ensure that they are?

Water can help us to find animal tracks

Look out for prints of wet pads on dry paving.
Impressions in mud or snow.

Different forms of water

Give the children opportunities to examine the following as they occur:

rain

ice

dew

frost (frozen dew)

mist (a cloud near the ground)

snow

Where does water go?

Let the children explore to discover:
water soaking into the ground
water rising from the ground into a stream
a stream running into a river which runs to the sea
water running off roofs into gutters, down drain pipes, into drains and then into sewers

Set up a bottle garden to show the water cycle in miniature

What lives and grows in water?

Find out by pond dipping.
Use pictures of water plants and pictures of water animals. Set up a classroom aquarium.

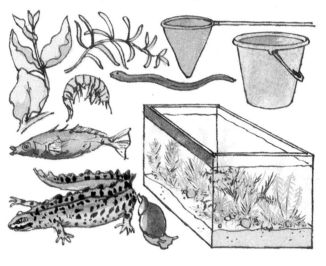

Words and records

puddle	waterfall	pond snails
gutter	rain	newts
water butt	ice	shrimps
stream	snow	tadpoles
ditch	frost	duckweed
river	dew	pondweed
canal	mist	bucket
reservoir	drizzle	aquarium
pond	downpour	net
sea	shower	gravel

much	flowing	floating
little	swirling	submerged
shallow	crashing	waves
deep	rushing	
moving	stagnant	
still		

We looked for water

Still water	Moving water
playground puddles Mrs Brown's water butt.	mill stream

Pooh sticks

	Ditch	Stream	River
10 seconds	0·5 m		
20 seconds	1·0 m		
30 seconds	1·5 m		

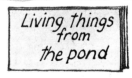

Living things from the pond

Ideas children can meet

Movement, stillness and depth.
Force of water carries things along.
Relationships between cloud types and rainfall.
Drying up (evaporation).
Water changes materials.
Water provides suitable living conditions for some plants and animals.
Water exists in different forms.

Compare appearances

Compare girls and boys in the class.
Who might be sisters or brothers?
Discuss the likeness between relatives.
Compare the appearance of dolls.

Compare size

Is the biggest child the oldest?

Compare heights. Who is tallest; who is shortest?
Compare length of limbs, head size, hand spans,
arm spans and length of pace.

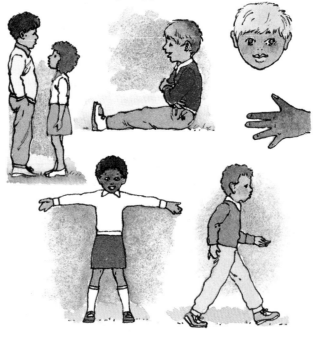

Compare hair and eyes

Make block graphs to show the different hair colours
and types and eye colours in the class.

Hair colour										
brown										
blond										
black										
red										
grey										

Dressing dolls

Match clothes to dolls according to:
size
weather conditions
occupations and activities such as
a Brownie meeting
swimming
helping in the garden
helping in the kitchen
going to a Christmas party

Making things that are needed gives children spatial experience and introduces technology.

Make a wardrobe

Use three cardboard boxes and cover with Fablon. It should be big enough to hold dolls' clothes.

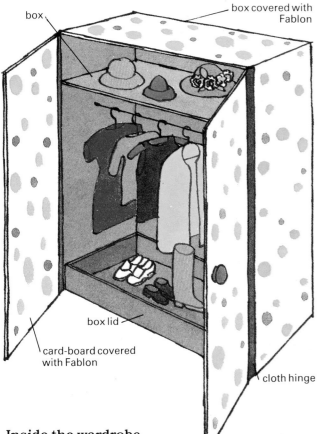

Inside the wardrobe

Coathangers are needed for holding coats, dresses, skirts and trousers. Make hangers for dresses and coats with bent wire.
Special hangers are needed for skirts and trousers. Make a balsa strip hanger.
Improve the design by adding map pins to the ends to hold clothes in position.

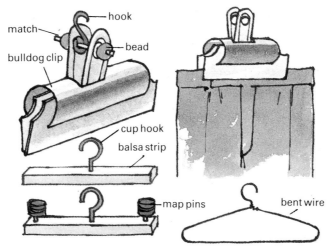

Investigate clothing materials

Look at different patterns, colours and textures. Investigate ways of cutting materials. How does this alter them?

Will water soak into fabric? Try various fabrics. Do they stretch or tear? Test the strength of fasteners.

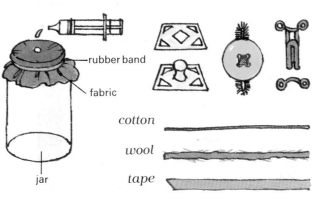

cotton

wool

tape

Words and records

centimetres	tall	dress
decimetres	short	slip
metres	umbrella	pants
fair	absorb	trousers
dark	permeable	shirt
straight	impermeable	T-shirt
curly	stretch	shoes

Chart the order of dressing and undressing.

Ideas children can meet

Length
The relationship of one thing to another: for example, a dress to a doll; a coathanger to a dress. One-to-one correspondence.
The relative nature of size: for instance, the wardrobe must be large enough to hold clothes.
Absorbency
Permeability
Impermeability
The relative nature of strength: for example, tape is stronger than cotton and weaker than rope.
Technology – making an article that is needed, for example, coat hangers.
Improving on a first design.

Hygiene – the home bay as a bathroom

Collect and display the things that are needed.

Let children find out by testing

Get them to wash their hands in different temperatures of water and record the results.

What is in the water	Cold water	Warm water
No soap		
Toilet soap		
Soap powder		

Activities with dolls

Bathtime, hair care and dental care can be demonstrated using dolls. What must be done and in what order?

Washing dolls' clothes – the home bay as a kitchen

How much water can different materials soak up (absorb). Find out by weighing them dry then wet. Get water out by wringing, squeezing, shaking and twirling them around. Which seems best? Now wash some garments and keep a record.

Kind of soap	Cold water	Very warm water
No soap		
Soap powder		
Soap powder and soda		

Drying material

How long do they take to dry when hung:

opened out in moving air? bunched up in moving air? opened out in still air?

 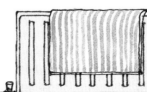

folded in quarters in still air? on a radiator?

Feeding our family in the kitchen

Collect pictures and labels of foods from animals.

Make a table of foods from plants.

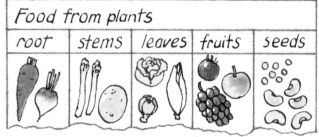

Food from plants				
root	stems	leaves	fruits	seeds

Tasting trials

Try milk, tea, coffee, vinegar, lemon, jam, butter, salty water, acid drops. Make a table.

Sweet	Sour	Salty	Bitter

Eating times and cooking

breakfast   dinner   tea   supper

Cooking involves measuring, mixing, heating and cooling solids and liquids.

The home bay as a bedroom

Which bedclothes keep the patient warm?

Wrap up Coke cans of hot water in different materials to test their insulation qualities. Record the temperature fall over a period of half-an-hour. Which material is best?

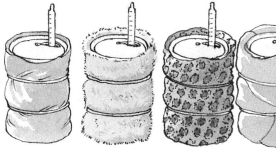

| sheet | woollen blanket | cellular blanket | eiderdown or duvet |

Practise using thermometers

Take the temperature of patients

under the tongue and under the armpit.

Take the temperature of the bedroom with:

window open   window closed

Playing doctors and nurses

*Telephone
for the doctor.*

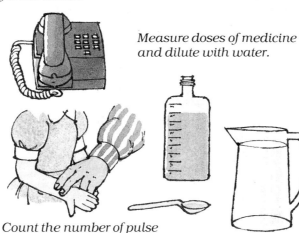

Measure doses of medicine and dilute with water.

Count the number of pulse beats in a minute.

Count the number of heart beats in a minute using a stethoscope.

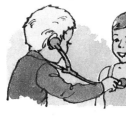

Words

clean	dry	tongue
dirty	soak	squeeze
germs	saturated	shake
cold	face	wring
warm	hands	towel
hot	hair	soap
liquid	teeth	soap powder
solid	arms	soap flakes
powder	legs	bath
flakes	feet	bowl
wet	nails	basin

flannel	temperature	telephone
nailbrush	medicine	doctor
toothbrush	pulse	nurse
hairbrush	stopwatch	
bath cubes	windy	
soda bottle	sunny	
ventilation	hot	
fresh air	cold	
thermometer	stethoscope	

Names of foods
    fruits
      vegetables
    cereals
    parts of plants
    things to taste
    flavours
      cooking utensils
      bedclothes

Ideas children can meet

Good health (keeping well).
Illness
Germs live in dirty places and are dangerous.
Poisons are dangerous.
Water from certain sources is better for washing.
Certain substances improve water's washing power.
Some environmental conditions speed up drying.
Saturation
Extraction
Food keeps people alive.
Foods have different flavours and colours.
People have food preferences.
Use of clinical thermometers.
Animals eat plants.
Animals eat other animals.
We eat animals and plants.
We could not live without plants.
Measurement of mass, volume, time, hotness and coldness
Intervals of time
Reference points of time
Ventilation
Insulation

Let children explore balance

Who can balance for the longest on a brick?

Who can walk furthest down the corridor balancing a book on his or her head?

Who can balance the longest on his or her head?

For how long can you balance a ball on your feet?

Can the children find their balancing point?

Who can travel furthest keeping on a chalk line?

Who can balance on tip toe the longest?

Who can balance
a walking stick
a broom
a wicker basket?

Try balancing on a see-saw and a rocker

How can a big child balance a small child?

The law of the see-saw

Children will soon begin to sense the relationship between the mass at one end and its distance from the balancing point, and the mass at the other end and its distance from the balancing point. That is, a heavy object on one side of the balancing point can be balanced by a lighter object further away from the balancing point on the other side.

Make a small see-saw

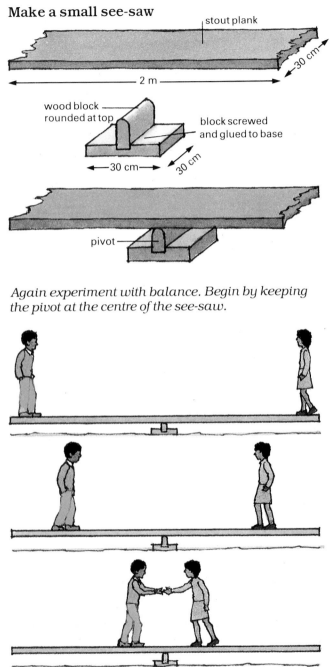

Again experiment with balance. Begin by keeping the pivot at the centre of the see-saw.

Can two of you balance one?

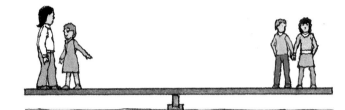

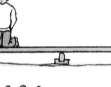

How else can you balance?

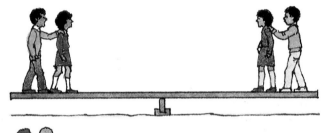

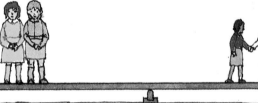

Now put the pivot off centre.

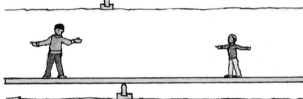

Try balancing things on your see-saw

Try roughly equal loads.

Try to balance unequal loads. What do you notice about their positions?

Explore balance on a smaller scale

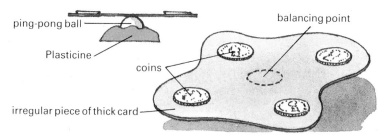

Try varying the position of the pivot to get a balance with unequal loads.

Make a pivot with Plasticine and a ping-pong ball. Find the balancing point.

ping-pong ball

Plasticine

balancing point

coins

irregular piece of thick card

Make some balancing toys

Does the top balance and spin better when the card is placed high on the pencil?

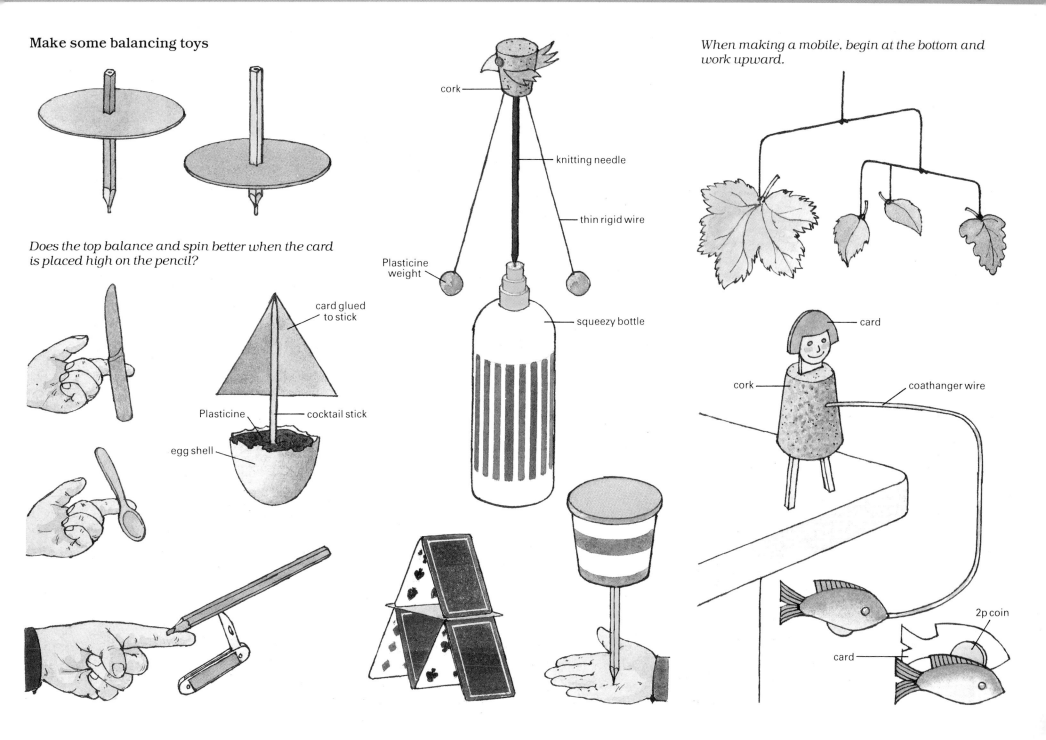

cork

knitting needle

thin rigid wire

Plasticine weight

squeezy bottle

card glued to stick

cocktail stick

Plasticine

egg shell

When making a mobile, begin at the bottom and work upward.

card

cork

coathanger wire

2p coin

card

Drawing and painting them

Make drawings and paintings of things that fly. Cut pictures from papers and magazines and mount them.

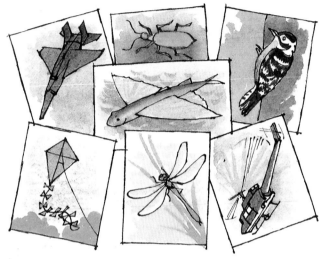

Look at seeds and fruits that fall and spin

sycamore   maple   ash

Try dropping them indoors.
Try dropping them outdoors on a windy day.

What can fly?

Collect things that can be made to fly through the air – paper plates, milk bottle tops, for example. Who can throw a paper plate furthest?

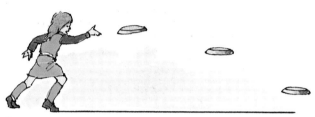

Try with a Frisbee.

Who can flick a milk bottle top furthest?

Make a paper spinner

Use a piece of writing paper.
Measure and cut it like this.

9 cm

12 cm

10 cm

3 cm

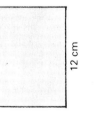

Fold it to make the spinner.

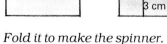

paper clip

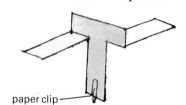

Make a paper glider

Use A4 paper. An old telephone directory will do.

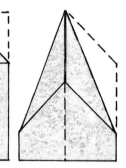
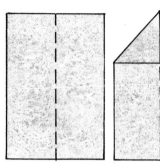

1 Fold in half, then open out again.
2 Fold the corners over.
3 Fold again as shown.

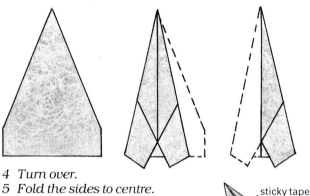

4 Turn over.
5 Fold the sides to centre.
6 Fold in half.
7 Hold the centre fold and open out.

sticky tape

How far will it glide?
Try adding a paper-clip nose-weight to the glider.
What happens?

Make a kite

1 Use a ceiling tile.
2 Find the centre and mark it.
3 Mark a spot 12 cm above the centre.
4 Make a hole through both these marks.
5 Thread string through and fasten to two buttons.
6 Fix a towing line to the string. Stick paper streamers to the base.

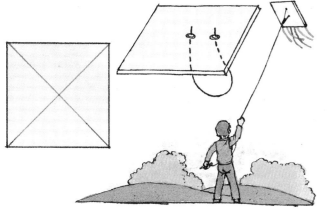

Make parachutes

Try using a handkerchief, thin plastic or tissue paper to make the canopy.
Try using big canopies and smaller canopies.
Try attaching different loads – for example, toy cars, toy animals.

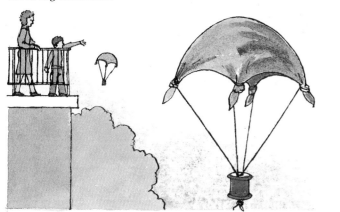

Make a windmill

1 Use paper 10 cm square.
2 Draw diagonals to mark the centre.
3 Mark five dots as in the picture.
4 Stick a pin through each dot.
5 Cut along the diagonals almost to the centre.
6 Bring the corners of the windmill together, to meet at the centre. Put a pin through all five holes.
7 Use a bead and a piece of balsa wood to mount the windmill.

Run with the windmill.

Is there a difference if you make it as above?

Make a jet balloon

How far will it travel?

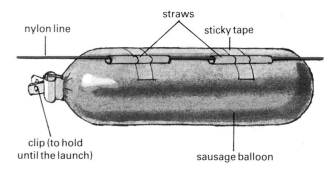

straws
nylon line
sticky tape
clip (to hold until the launch)
sausage balloon

Make a hovercraft

Make a hole in a polystyrene tray large enough to take a toilet roll tube. Push a length of tube into the hole.

piece of toilet roll tube
inverted polystyrene tray

Blow on the hovercraft to make it hover.

What you need

wirecutter and stripper

crocodile clips

bare the ends

screwdriver

five MES bulbs (screw in type)

five MES (screw) bulbholders

insulated wire

Make some switches

springy piece of steel

drawing pin

Use the switch to make the light flash.

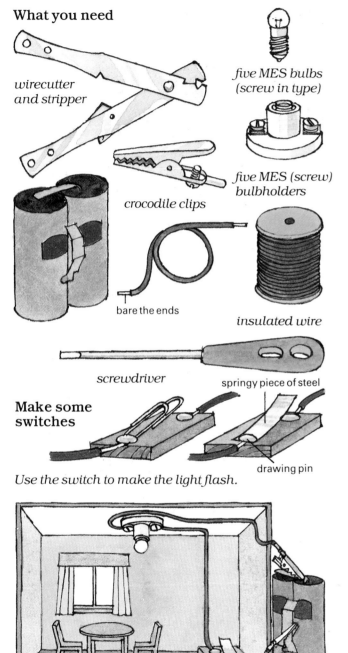

What will electricity pass through?

Indoors

Outdoors

Make a model lighthouse

jam-jar

washing-up liquid container

Make eyes for David and Goliath

Use one battery to light two bulbs

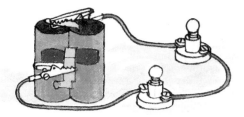

Try two different circuits. Which circuit gives the brighter light?

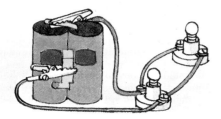

Make a monster with eyes that light up

Make an electromagnet

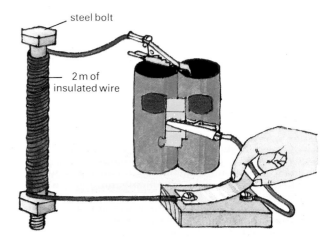

steel bolt

2 m of insulated wire

Make sure you use a switch because electromagnets run down batteries quickly.

What will the electromagnet pick up?

Put lights in a toy theatre

Put lights on a toy car

Collect and display lots of transparent things

How easy is it to see through all the objects in the collection?

Is all glass transparent? What about rippled glass, glass marbles, glass from a reflector, engraved glass?

Plastic bags and lunch boxes lose their transparency with age because their surfaces become scratched.

Dirt and grease also affect the transparency of an object.

Discuss the differences between transparent, translucent and opaque objects.

How transparent?

Through how many layers of polythene can the picture still be seen?
How many layers must there be before the picture disappears?

A see-through display

Make a range of coloured solutions in various shaped bottles, using food colourings. What happens if the bottles overlap?

Lenses

Collect some lenses from old spectacles. Hold them up to throw an image of a window on to a sheet of card. Note that the image is inverted.

Bubbles

Blow some bubbles. Are they transparent? What colours can be seen in them? Try square bubble frames as well as round ones.

See-through paintings

Paint large pictures on the windows. Draw the outlines with chalk and fill them in with powder paints mixed with cold-water paste. The pictures will wash off easily.

Make a collection of shiny things

Collect utensils, pots and pans, ornaments, Christmas decorations, rocks and minerals, jewellery, mirrors, coins. Blow bubbles.

In which ones can children see their faces? Make some drawings.

Sort the objects: for example, metallic and non-metallic; very shiny and dull; those that reflect faces and those that do not.

Play with mirrors

Does your reflection do what you do? Touch your eye. Touch your nose. Put your hands on your head.

Look at the sky.

Look behind you.

Look round corners.

Look over walls.

Kaleidoscope

Hinge two mirrors together with sticky tape. Vary the angle between the mirrors. How many images can you see?

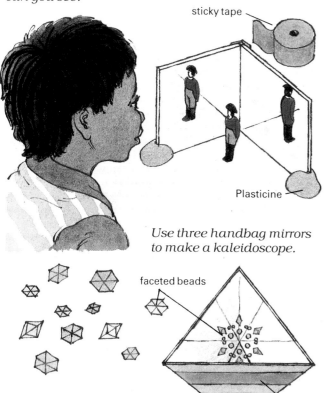

Use three handbag mirrors to make a kaleidoscope.

Two kinds of kaleidoscope are available.

Puff into the end of a kaleidoscope to see the mirrors cloud up.

Periscope

Cut a cube of wood diagonally into two pieces. Fix each piece to two strips of wood, as shown in the diagram. Glue a small handbag mirror to each piece of wood.

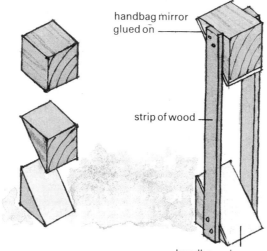

Look over the tops of walls and around corners. Spy for people coming up the corridor.

More repeated images

Set up two mirrors facing each other and place an object between them. Peep over the top of one mirror into the other.

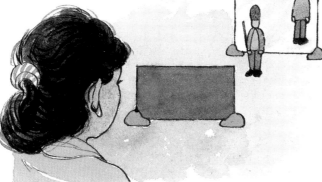

Try some tricks

Draw patterns and figures like these. Hold a curved mirror over them in various ways to make them fatter, thinner, larger, smaller — or disappear! Can you get the images to repeat?

Some of the main ideas to emerge from a study of shiny things are:
Shiny surfaces reflect light well.
A mirror image is the opposite way to the object (lateral inversion).
Curved shiny surfaces distort images.
Putting two mirrors together multiplies the images.
Two mirrors at an angle produce a 'kaleidoscope' effect.

Books for teachers
Early Experiences, Science 5/13, Macdonald

Ourselves, Science 5/13, Macdonald

Early Explorations, Science 5/13, Macdonald

Science for Children with Learning Difficulties,
Learning Through Science, Macdonald

Books for children
Read and Do series
Authors: Doug Kincaid and Peter Coles
Publishers: Arnold-Wheaton

Eyes and Looking
Ears and Hearing
Taste and Smell
Touch and Feel
Hot and Cold
Wet and Dry
Light and Dark
Quiet and Loud

Starters Science
Author: Albert James
Publishers: Macdonald

Wheels
Strong and Weak
Hot and Cold
Drips and Drops
Noises
Light and Shadows
Floating Things
Batteries and Bulbs
Balancing Things
Wet and Dry

Suppliers of apparatus and materials
E.J. Arnold & Son Ltd
Dewsbury Road
Leeds LS11 5TD
Telephone: 0532 772112

Griffin & George Ltd
Bishops Meadow Road
Loughborough
Leicestershire LE11 0RG
Telephone: 0509 233344

Philip Harris Ltd
Lynn Lane
Shenstone
Staffordshire WS14 0EE
Telephone: 0543 480077

Osmiroid International Ltd
Fareham Road
Gosport
Hampshire PO13 0AL
Telephone: 0329 232345